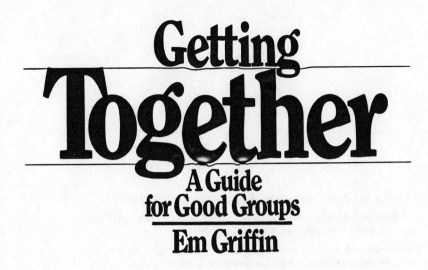

Getting Together

A Guide for Good Groups

Em Griffin

InterVarsity Press
Downers Grove
Illinois 605 5

InterVarsity Press is the book-publishing division of Inter-Varsity Christian Fellowship, a student movement active on campus at hundreds of universities, colleges and schools of nursing. For information about local and regional activities, write IVCF, 233 Langdon St., Madison, WI 53703.

Distributed in Canada through InterVarsity Press, 1875 Leslie St., Unit 10, Don Mills, Ontario M3B 2M5, Canada.

Chapter three was first published in Eternity (May 1977) under the title "Why Some People Become Leaders." Chapter five was first published in Leadership (Winter 1981) under the title "The Greening of a Discussion Leader." Chapter six was first published in Leadership (Spring 1980) under the title "Self-Disclosure: How Far Should a Leader Go?"

Louise White's poem from W. H. Fitts, The Experience of Psychotherapy © 1965; reprinted by permission of D. Van Nostrand Co., pp. 55-56.

Cover cartoon: © Bill Maul. Reprinted by permission of Saturday Review.

ISBN 0-87784-390-2

Printed in the United States of America

Library of Congress Cataloging in Publication Data

Griffin, Emory A.
        Getting together.

        Includes bibliographical references.
        1. Small groups.   2. Social group work.
3. Church group work.   I. Title.
HM131.G648   302.3'4   82-7131
ISBN 0-87784-390-2   AACR2

17 16 15 14 13 12 11 10 9 8 7 6 5 4 3
95 94 93 92 91 90 89 88 87 86 85 84

Introduction

I'm excited about groups. They have such potential for good. That optimism seems natural since I've just completed a book about groups and group leadership. After three long years this somewhat slothful author has finished the text, made most of the changes my editor suggested and proofread the galleys. I've pulled together the footnotes (an onerous task), selected the cartoons (an enjoyable task) and only this preface remains before it is all in the hands of my publisher. After all that I'd *better* be bullish on groups.

But my special enthusiasm comes not from words on a page but from people banded together for common purposes. I've just returned from a meeting of the Westwood Food Co-op. That name may be devoid of meaning for you, but for me it calls up images of a year's work and prayer. With a Christian coworker, I've been trying to serve the tenants of a low-income housing project in the inner city. The area is the exact antithesis of my own highly educated, white, wealthy suburb. Yet a number of these folks have accepted me as a friend, and we've worked jointly to try to improve their quality of life. The food co-op is a small, but significant, group effort in that direction. The story of its formation provides a good introduction to the topics of this book and also gives you an initial glimpse of who I am. I think you have a right to know the fellow behind the words.

The Westwood Food Co-op has all the features of the good group laid out in chapter one. It's a cohesive association that has a specific purpose, and everyone knows the part they are supposed to play.

The co-op was the brainchild of the people who live in Westwood. My friend Jessie and I spent six months knocking on doors, getting to know the people, listening to their story. We then surveyed the community to determine the overriding needs. The high cost of food was at the top of the list. (Identifying needs is the theme of chapter two.)

Chapter three looks at different approaches to leadership. Jessie and I each had to figure out how we could best meet the needs of the people. We are very different. I became the resource person for information on food wholesalers. I proposed a distribution system and pushed for an ultimate decision on whether or not to give the plan a try. In short, my leadership was aimed at moving the group toward its goal. Jessie was the encourager, sympathizer, reconciler. Her leadership was geared to holding the group together. It was a good mix.

Once the group was formed we discovered that people had joined for a variety of reasons: some to accomplish a task, some to build relationships and some to have influence. These three main categories parallel parts one, two and three of this book.

The stated task of our group was to get high-quality food as cheaply as possible. We spent a number of meetings trying to decide the best way to do this. Chapter four looks at the pros and cons of four methods of decision making. At one time or another we used them all. Chapter five is a nuts-and-bolts presentation on how to lead a discussion in a way that folks will feel free to express what they're really thinking. This was an important skill for me to have at Westwood. Some people were hesitant to say how much they wanted to spend, whether or not they would work distributing the food and what they thought about the quality after it came.

Although low price was a factor to everybody, the warmth of human companionship was most important to some. They placed a high premium on the relationships that grew out of working together. A Black mother traded her secret for cooking collard greens for a Chicano mother's recipe for guacamole. It led to further sharing on child rearing, illnesses and the frustrations of looking for a job. Chapter six in the relationship section deals with appropriate self-disclosure, and chapter seven examines ways to handle conflict—a must for developing closer ties. We've had plenty of conflict from within and without. The government administrator of the housing project wanted to put the co-op out of business because he felt it would threaten existing charity programs in the city. One of the tenants saw the co-op as an ideal occasion to take the administrator to court, and railed against the co-op members who had no stomach for legal action.

The influence section of the book focuses on the desire of group members to have a mutual impact on each other's lives. I've learned that being poor is not just a matter of having no money. It means being powerless! At least a few joined the co-op so that Westwood tenants might have some control over their own destiny. Along with Jessie and me, they wanted to have an impact on the whole community. Chapter eight describes three ways people are persuaded: compliance, identification, internalization. We've aimed for internalization, desiring that people would join the co-op not through pressure or winsome personality but because they were convinced it would benefit them.

A question-answer format in chapter nine is used to cover

deviance. And the co-op has had a bit of that at ordering time. One family refuses to round off their purchase to even amounts. They request thirteen pounds of potatoes, seventeen apples, two and a half pounds of ground round. Chapter ten centers on the power of expectation. When I assumed no one could handle the ordering and bookkeeping except me, there were no volunteers. When it dawned on me that the users were quite capable of performing these functions, two people immediately came forward.

The final chapter of the book presents personal insights that I've culled from these opportunities. I use the lives of biblical leaders to illustrate my ideas. I am a Christian and assume that most of my readers will share this concern for Christ and his kingdom. It's also the reason I wrote this book.

I don't want to leave the impression that all of the truths presented in this book come from one man's experience. I've tried to base my advice on the most solid theory in the field. Students of group dynamics will recognize McClelland's theory of motivation, Fiedler's contingency model, Festinger's theory of informal social communication, Altman and Taylor's social penetration theory and many more embedded in the text. My debt to these researchers can be pursued through the footnotes. But I've worked to avoid using the jargon of the field so the practitioner can get the most out of the book. Let's face it, if what I've written doesn't help you work better with others, I've failed.

There's one other issue I want to speak to. Occasionally I run across believers who are uneasy applying principles of group dynamics to their Christian group. "What you say may be O.K. in a secular situation," they say. "But our group operates under the guidance of the Holy Spirit, so we don't need that stuff." Apparently they feel that when people commit their lives to Jesus Christ they somehow put their humanity in the attic. I can only say that twenty years of working with Christian groups give me no indication that principles of human behavior apply only to non-Christians. Truth is truth wherever it's found—in Scripture, through our own experience or in the social science laboratory. We don't need to be afraid of what we discover through systematic investigation. The facts are benign. All truth is God's truth.

Although writing is a solitary activity, many people have shaped the finished product. My thanks goes to Carol Balow for having the patience to decipher my handwritten scrawl and convert it to typescript with accepted spelling.

Then there's a group of eight people who really aren't a group. Technically speaking, a group is made up of people who come together at the same time and have a psychological effect on each other. These people have never been face to face. In fact no one of them knows more than three of the others. Yet I often think of them collectively because they are friends who love me, pray for me, encourage me and care so much that they're willing to see the dark side of Em Griffin and not get scared off. Instead they stick close to me and help me change. That's true friendship, and I'm grateful to Bill, Lee, Arlene, Butch, Jessie, Sally, Glen and another Bill for that gift. You'll meet some of them in these pages.

Finally, it is with great delight that I publicly proclaim my love and debt to the group that holds the greatest meaning for me —my family. Sharon and Jim are "people persons" who stimulate me with their acute social perception, sense of humor and zest for life. No father could wish for a finer daughter or son. My wife Jean has been my model for social compassion, intellectual curiosity and commitment to excellence. Her depth of love has freed me to take the risk of reaching out to other people. Without the encouragement of these three, writing this book would have been a joyless task.

Part One

A
First
Look

1

The
Good
Group

It is the fifth of July. Every bone in my body is weary. My arm muscles shriek in protest even as I write. Yesterday I worked together with a dozen other folks to sell pop at our community's all-day Fourth of July celebration. A ton of ice and four thousand cans later, midnight came. Everyone was beat, but no one wanted to go home. It was a good time. We were a good group.

The official label of our group is the Glen Ellyn Young Life Committee. Our overall aim is to supervise and support the Christian outreach of Young Life to teen-agers in our community. Our specific goal yesterday was to raise a thousand dollars in scholarships to send students to camp. Not only did we accomplish our task, we also had a great time. As one gal put it, "If the Young Life club ever folds, I'd want to stay together with these people and work for some other cause."

The committee is not perfect. But it gives me a springboard

to bounce off some principles for good groups. Koinonia fellowship, church board or Alcoholics Anonymous—there are some qualities that all groups need if they're going to be effective. This will take up the rest of this chapter. But these common features aren't the whole picture. The church board with a job of figuring out the annual budget should look different from a sharing group aiming at close relationships. And neither would capture the genius of an AA group trying to help members conquer drinking problems. In the next chapter I will sketch the special features of each.

All for One and One for All

To paraphrase the rhyme about the girl with the curl: "When groups are good, they are very, very good. And when they are bad, they are horrid." What do the very good ones look like?

The good group has cohesiveness. Folks come early and stay late. Most importantly, they come. High absenteeism is the mark of a noncohesive group. Nothing can kill a group spirit quicker than to have members look around at empty chairs and realize that others are voting by their absence. Some of the couples on the Young Life Committee had long-standing commitments to be out of town on the Fourth, but everyone else was there. We originally signed up for three-hour shifts but soon disregarded the schedule because everyone worked the whole time. As for me, I was excited at how well things were going and was afraid I might miss something if I left.

Cohesiveness involves a sense of group identity, a feeling of we-ness. I don't think any of us would say we're *on* the Young Life Committee. We *are* the YL Committee. In case any of the thousands of people in the park wouldn't know that, we all wore sun visors with the logo Υ on the brim. Groups that stick together usually have T-shirts, jackets, rings, buttons or some other symbol that proudly proclaims a member's allegiance. This is hard to engineer. You can come up with a spiffy uniform idea or a clever sweatshirt design. You can give them away free. But if

16

Drawing by Dana Fradon; © 1976, The New Yorker Magazine, Inc.

"Why, this broth we made is magnificent!"

members aren't attracted to the group, the clothes will remain unworn in the closet.

My son once commented on the drawing power of our group. Jim and I were talking about human nature. I asked him whether he thought people were basically good or bad. He replied that sometimes he was convinced that people were rotten to the core but that often he saw a tremendous capacity for goodness. I was pleased that he didn't have a simplistic view. But I pursued the issue. When was one of the times he was impressed with human potential? "When I see you together with the Seavoys, Johansens, Debarrs and Sonesons," he said. Even though Jim is not on the committee, he has picked up the fact that we are attracted to one another and enjoy each other's presence. That's cohesiveness.

When a group has hung tightly together over a period of time, it usually develops some shared experiences or fantasies that members will fondly relive. For us, one such experience was an overnight retreat at a lakeside cabin. We played Spook. It's a form of hide-and-seek where one person, unknown to the rest of the group, is "it." The others try to figure out who the person is and then join him. When you find the spook you stay quietly together until the whole group is there. The game is complicated by the fact that it's played in the dark. It was a cloudy night by the lake, far from the reflected glow of the city lights. You literally could not see your hand in front of your face. The last person hunted in vain and finally turned on the lights. He saw nine of us huddled together in the shower stall. Then someone turned on the water. Here was a college professor, telephone company executive, advertising copywriter, mother of three, kindergarten teacher—all laughing uproariously with water dripping down their faces. That story has been related countless times.

Sometimes cohesiveness shows in the form of a group fantasy. John Stewart suggests that a relationship between two people is like a spiritual child with an existence all its own. Through nourishment the child (that is, the relationship) will develop to maturity. Or we can starve and ignore it so the child's growth is stunted or maimed. It's a nice analogy, and in one course it captured my students' imagination. They began talking about all the invisible kids running around in our midst. Of course the idea is sheer fantasy. But that's part of its charm. As one of the girls and I drew close we extended the fantasy to the point of giving our spiritual child a name, talking about how to nurture it and wondering about its condition ten years down the road. Some would call that foolishness. But it's a sign of cohesiveness. We are still close.

Cohesiveness does not mean the absence of conflict. In fact there's strong evidence to the contrary. When people are close, they have the resources to deal with conflict. So they allow it to surface. We've had some real shoot-outs at our YL Committee meetings. It took two hours of wrangling to determine the proportions of Coke, Tab and Sprite to order. (We got too much Tab. Apparently weight watching is out on national holidays.) When the bonds are weak, however, people seem to sense that disagreement would fracture the group, so everyone stays "nicey-nicey."

One final word. There's some good news and bad news about cohesion. The good news is obvious. The closer a group is, the more it serves the needs of its members and the harder members will work to make it go. The bad news is more subtle. The more cohesive a group, the harder it is to get into—and out of. To outsiders it may seem snobbish or cliquish. This can be a problem for people meeting in the name of Jesus Christ. We don't want to exclude anyone from our fellowship, yet our in-jokes, language of Zion and common experiences may throw up barriers that are tough to crack. There's no easy answer to this problem. The very closeness that makes the group attractive to its members can exclude outsiders. If we let everyone in without any standards for membership, the group will lose its uniqueness and attraction. But if we draw the lines too tightly, we alienate those who want and need to belong. We need to strike the balance of the early church. "Behold how they love one another," exclaimed outsiders. Yet when they opted to join they were welcomed with open arms. How to stay cohesive with a fluid membership? If you figure it out, drop me a line.

A Place for Everyone

I got a call from a fellow about a year ago asking if he could visit a Young Life Committee meeting. We're always looking out for new blood, so I said, "Sure." Jeanie and I picked him up, and on the way to the session he pumped me with a number of questions. Suddenly he asked, "What's your function?" Jeanie and I still chuckle about the forthrightness of his query. Here's a guy I don't even know asking me to define my worth in the group by outlining a job description, a role. But even though it struck me as cold and impersonal, the idea that I filled a particular slot in the organization made sense.

In good groups, people know where they fit. They occupy a comfortable niche. That doesn't mean they're complacent—just that they and everybody concerned know what to expect from them. This meshing doesn't always come fast or easy. Often folks are in a state of flux as a group forms.

"What am I doing here?"

"Who's this guy? What does he do?"

"Where do I fit in?"

"How do I proceed?"

It's the uncertainty that's so wearing. Often people will seem bored when a group starts. Don't be taken in by the apparent lethargy. It's usually a cover-up for tension. The anxiety dissipates when their role gets hammered out by the group. Once they know their slot they're free to take on almost any task.

I often play a game with my students to show the importance of roles in group communication. I seat them in a circle and affix a 3″ x 5″ card to their foreheads. (Hair clips or rubber bands around the head work better than thumbtacks.) I give every student a designation and a way to treat that person. Some of the signs might say:

Smart. (Listen to me.)

Sexy. (Flirt with me.)

Pushy. (Resist me.)

Players in the game can see everyone's role but their own. I then assign a discussion topic and let the group go to it. The first ten minutes is agony. The discussion is stilted, most of the comments inane. Their real energy is going into discovering who they are. But as things get sorted out the ideas become more valuable. People may not like the role assigned to them, but it's always more comfortable than not knowing. Occasionally

20

I use a card that merely has a large question mark on it. The group is in a quandary on how to respond. As a result that person receives conflicting cues and doesn't know how to act. I don't do it often because I don't like to see people get frustrated, which happens if you don't let roles emerge.

It took our Young Life group over a year to arrive at meaningful roles. Part of this was my fault. I had called the group together in the first place but failed to let them know the specific goals of the committee. I was long on excitement, short on direction. More on this in a minute. That sorting-out period was long and tedious, but once it occurred we ended up with people filling slots that most good groups seem to have. These included:

The Mover—the "can do" person who rolls up her sleeves and gets to work. Our mover runs her own wallpaper business. At 5′ 2″ and 95 lbs., she can hang five rolls while someone else is just beginning to stir the paste.

The Clown—the jokester who keeps things from getting too serious. I do this in other groups, but it's not my function with

Reprinted with permission from The Saturday Evening Post Company © 1980

"Capt'n! One of the mates here has a suggestion!"

these people. We've got one who leaves us on the floor.

The Skeptic—the one who raises tough questions just about the time the group's ready to get carried away. If you're a *Winnie the Pooh* fan, you can think of this person as the group's Eeyore. Often maligned, her doubts serve a valuable function.

The Technician—the fellow who has expertise where you need it most. Sometimes this role floats from person to person as the task of the group changes. In our case it shifts between a man who has the financial know-how to figure out the Young Life accounting system and the former club leader who knows how to help our college volunteers work with high-school students.

The Encourager—the warm soul who builds up others and makes them feel valuable. He or she is good at smoothing ruffled feathers and soothing bruised egos. We have a woman who does a super job at this.

The Deviant—the person who's different. He or she may hold back or suggest things that are off the wall. This might not seem like a helpful role, but read on. When you get to the chapter on deviance, you'll discover that *every* good group needs one.

The Nice Guy—the foot soldier who does what is asked without grumbling. Not an initiator but someone with a sense of responsibility. Our group has at least three people who fit that description. They have lifted many cases of pop and chilled a lot of ice.

The Leader—that's a role too, often the last to emerge. You'll read more in chapter two about the requirements of specific types of leadership. Suffice to say that every group needs at least one.

You may have noticed that the list does not include Spiritual Giant. We don't have any Saint Francis of Assisi look-alike. As it turns out, that's an advantage. Each member offers Christian input. This leads us to the final mark of a good group—a common purpose.

You Wonder Why I Called This Meeting
People come together to meet a variety of needs. Our Young Life

Committee is no exception. At least one couple is grateful that their teen-ager met Christ through Young Life. They see their service on the committee as a way of having an impact on the community. (A need for power.) A second couple comes because they have developed close ties within the group. When the man received a job offer out of town, the loss of these friendships became a significant factor in making a decision. (A need for affiliation.) Yet another couple sees the committee as providing a necessary support for the actual club work with kids. They get a sense of accomplishment in being the people behind the scenes who train the volunteer leaders. (A need for achievement.)

For members to come with different internal needs doesn't hurt the group. In fact, one sign of a healthy organization is that it meets a mixture of motives under the same umbrella. To achieve this there has to be a common perception of what the group is about. This is where I fell short. When I first got eight couples together to form a Young Life committee, I was too vague about its purpose. I suppose I was afraid that a detailed bill of particulars would drive everybody away. So I mouthed some generalities about being a support group for Young Life within the community. That was a mistake. At least one man assumed that the sole purpose was to be a board of reference, to answer parents' questions when they contacted him. When he found out that others expected him to raise funds, he took a hike. Another woman was quite comfortable with fund raising but panicked at the spiritual responsibility of membership. She felt threatened when others prayed for students by name. It offended her concept of privacy.

Over the years we've developed a common commitment to some specific goals such as:

1. To raise money for Young Life.
2. To train and supervise volunteer leaders.
3. To pray for students.

If each member articulates roughly similar group goals, you know you're on the right track. It's even better when each person feels a personal stake in the success or failure of the group. The term *ownership* nicely describes that commitment. When I make the group's aim my own personal goal, I'm tied in with something bigger than myself. Paul's analogy of the body of Christ in 1 Corinthians 12 nicely picks up that imagery. In addition to selling soft drinks, the committee raffled off a handsewn quilt. The ladies on the committee each sewed a square. Lest you think we're a chauvinistic bunch, I worked with two other men cutting out the patterns. But the yeoman's work was done by Marsha. She bought the material, traced the pattern, distributed the work, did a number of squares herself and assembled the final product. The quilt was lovely, but at first it looked like ticket sales were a flop. Marsha was naturally disappointed. A last day push brought a surge of contributions. When we hit five hundred, we were as excited for Marsha as we were for Young Life. That's ownership.

So cohesiveness, role differentiation and a common commitment are the signs of a good group. If that sounds a bit sociological to you—and it does strike me as a bit heavy on the jargon —try it from the human point of view. If people are close, know where they fit in and see the group's purpose in the same way, the group is likely a winner. Before we can say for sure, however, we need to check out the special requirements of task, relationship and influence groups. We'll take them in that order in the next chapter.

2

Scratching Where They Itch

Groups can be a pain! That may sound strange after having just read the previous chapter. But let's face it, who can't recall the frustration of trying to get everyone to agree or even just trying to get them together at the same time? There's the boredom that sets in while listening to the drone of the monopolizer. And it's a toss-up which grates me more—meaningless and idle chatter over stale refreshments or the stomach-wrenching conflict which erupts between two people who love the Lord but can't stand each other.

Because hassles like these are legion, many Christian leaders have grown cynical toward small groups. They share the jaundiced sentiments expressed in the following supposed truisms:

Too many cooks spoil the broth.

If you want something done, do it yourself.

Nothing is impossible until it is sent to a committee.

A camel is a horse put together by a committee.

"Would you scratch my back?"

But there are those rare times when a group of individuals coalesces into a single unit and produces an effect so dazzling that we blink in amazement. That occasional triumph holds forth the tantalizing prospect that group life can be beautiful. Why then is it so rare?

I think the answer has something to do with a leader's willingness to flex to the needs of the group. Many leaders are one-trick ponies. They have a set way of dealing with people. That's fine if their particular style happens to mesh with what the situation requires. But consistency isn't necessarily a virtue. What serves well in one case may not be helpful in another. Different groups have different needs.

There seems to be a group for almost every conceivable purpose in life. I'm a member of a pilot organization, a political lobby pushing world famine relief, an association of speech teachers, a tennis foursome, a church Bible study, a sharing fellowship of families, a group of hockey dads—just to mention a few. I suspect that each of you could come up with a list equally as varied. But despite the diversity of thousands of ongoing groups, almost

26

all of them can be lumped together in one of three categories. They exist either to accomplish a joint task, foster mutual relationships or influence members to change their behavior and attitudes.

Now of course there is no such thing as a pure task group, relationship group or influence group. All three go on in any collection of individuals, but it's helpful to classify each aggregate under its main purpose. If your main thrust is to get a job done, your group should look different from a group whose goal is fellowship. And if your purpose is to produce change, the group will take on yet another appearance.

The Task Group

Task groups form to accomplish a job which can't be done by one person alone. The classic example is the assembly line. Most workers don't have the know-how or resources to put together a car from scratch. But if you form a group composed of a good chassis man, a riveter, spray painter and so on, and organize them into an integrated unit, they can end up producing cars in greater quantity and quality than the same folks working by themselves. Note the word *can*. It's not automatic.

Task groups can be mental as well as physical. The goal of the group can be to arrive at a decision, solve a problem or reach a joint understanding of new material. The typical committee or council meeting is a group with a cognitive task.

We're quite familiar with task groups in our churches. The board of trustees, elders and deacons have goals to accomplish. Sunday-school classes and Bible studies which concentrate on historical information or scriptural content fall into this category. Their task is learning. Church staffs work together to plan and execute a program which includes everything from Sunday services and helping those in need, to getting out a newsletter or bulletin.

If you're working with a task group you need to raise certain questions:

□ What is the most effective style of leadership to organize our people?

□ What is the optimum size for our group?

□ Do all folks really share the same goal or is there a hidden agenda?

□ How can we draw out shy members to benefit from their ideas?

□ What method of decision making will give us a quality solution which members will support?

□ Can we allow diversity and disagreement in our midst?

Let's take a closer look at the church board preparing a budget. Why have a group tackle the issue in the first place? Why not let the financial officer do it alone? There are many possible answers. Certainly there will be a greater sense of ownership if the bottom-line figures come from the congregation rather than from a single accountant with a sharp pencil. The budget process is also an excellent training ground for future leaders. But most leaders would feel that the main reason for tossing the problem to a group is that they can do a better job together than they can working by themselves. The group is greater than the sum of its parts. If this isn't so, why bother? Who needs the hassle of late night meetings, arguments, scheduling problems and sending out minutes if it can be done another way?

Here's my image of what a good budgeting task force would look like.

1. *The group is small.* Five or seven people is about right. Fewer than five and you don't have enough resources to draw on. And four people can divide two against two. There's a similar problem with six. Once you hit eight or nine there won't be time for everyone to stick in their oar. Some people will feel shut out; subgroups will form. So five or seven is an ideal size for a decision-making body. If the task requires hitting the pavement —as in our Young Life pop sale—then you need more.

2. *The agenda is short.* Everyone should have a chance to have a say. That takes time. It's equally important that people

have an inclination to listen to one another. Both are necessary to have a high-fidelity exchange of ideas. I was recently at a ninety-minute meeting that had twenty-two topics scheduled for consideration. The group talked about three of them, got-talked *at* about another eight and then skipped eleven. A good budgetary meeting will consider a few key issues in depth—the percentages that will go to missions, salaries and necessary building repairs. The group will leave the nickel-and-dime housekeeping questions to the person in charge.

3. *The people are diverse.* It would be helpful to have a banker, accountant or broker on the board. But it's equally important to include a homemaker, laborer or educator. The more varied the background, outlook and temperament of the people, the better your chance of reaching sound decisions. Most leaders are scared of this kind of diversity. They appoint their friends and people with whom they can get along. As one pastor put it in a moment of candor; "My idea of an agreeable committee is one that agrees with me." That's too bad. We miss God's best if we limit a group's perspective to our own tunnel vision.

It's vital to get some folks who are task oriented and some who place more importance on relationships within the group. Without a few hard-driving, nose-to-the-grindstone types, the job will never get done. The group will flounder. But a committee made up entirely of steely eyed workaholics will quickly disintegrate under its own friction. You need the balance of a few warm souls who take time to smell the roses, tell a joke and show pictures of their kids. This is the social lubricant that will allow a group to work together over the long haul. The differences have gone by many names:

Task orientation vs. relationship orientation.

Concern for production vs. concern for people.

Work functions vs. maintenance functions.

Need for achievement vs. need for affiliation.

But no finding in the field of group dynamics is more clear.[1] A good group has a balance of both kinds of people

Balance is the key word when it comes to attitudes as well. Some folks are just naturally positive. They smile, agree and are pleasant to be around. Others tend to ask hard questions, see the problems with no solutions and in general cast a bit of gloom into the proceedings. You'd think it would be best to choose the former and dump the rest. Not so. A group does its best work when the positive and negative forces are in some kind of equilibrium. A two-to-one or three-to-one ratio of pluses over minuses seems to achieve the best results. Too much tension and you have schism. But too little and you end up with the pap that can only come from a group of yes men.

4. *The process moves in definite stages.* Different social researchers have analyzed hundreds of successful task groups to see if a pattern emerges. It does.[2] One man spotted three distinct phases. He labeled the first one *flight* to represent the members' reticence to get down to business. The second he called *fight* to signify the tough battle that was being waged over different ideas. *Unite* was the final stage, a time when opposing forces came together. Another investigator discovered the same basic movement. He titled the phases *forming, storming* and *norming.* He then picked up on the implementation of the group solution and called that *performing.* (These social scientists do have a penchant for rhyming.)

All agree that there's a period of orientation while people test the water, followed by a plunge into dispute. Conflict is smack-dab in the middle of a productive work group. Leaders who try to suppress disagreement do so at the group's peril. If the proportion of funds going to missions isn't worth some lively debate, what is?

Unfortunately, life is never simple. An effective task group requires a different style of leadership depending on which phase it's in. If members have no experience, don't know where they fit in and have little idea which way to go, they need to be told exactly what to do. After this shakedown period members begin to gain maturity. They move into the second phase where conflict comes to the fore. An iron-fisted hard-guy approach no longer works. In fact it irritates the problem. What's needed is a gentle relational touch that will help build bridges to people. Instead of telling people what to do, the leader needs to join with them, participating in their struggles. The uniting stage comes as a pleasant conclusion to the discord. But now the group needs someone to put wheels on their solution. A relational style would be self-indulgent at this point. What's best is a clear delegation of responsibility, a pat on the back and gentle but firm encouragement to get to it.

Can one person be that flexible? Some say no. It's not fair to ask time-oriented managers to chuck their performance check list so discouraged group members can have an empathic ear. Neither is it realistic to expect friendly counselors to become hard-driving taskmasters. Leopards can't change their spots. The solution? Match the leader with the situation. When you need to advance the troops come hell or high water, put Patton in charge. When the situation calls for a warm diplomatic approach, send Eisenhower. As the group moves from phase to phase, change leaders.[3]

Another approach buys the idea that one person can't do it all but calls for a less radical solution. Have two leaders: a task expert (usually the stated or official leader of the group) and a social-emotional specialist (to meet the personal needs of members).[4] While this might seem chaotic on an organizational chart, it often works well in practice. The traditional family is an excellent example. The father is the task leader, the mother the relational head. This implies no necessary subordination of one role to the other. The family needs both.

A third approach would challenge the assumption that one person can't do both. It's possible, so the argument goes, for a sensitive person to truly be a man for all seasons.[5] This is where I cast my lot. I don't claim it's easy, and probably not everyone can flex that much. But this is a section on the ideal group, and I believe that ideal leaders can offer encouragement to those who are down and give a kick in the rear to those who need direction —all at the same time. To do this well, they have to be aware of their own tendencies. I know that I tend to be a get-the-job-done type, so I have to fan the flame of my relational nature lest I quench the spirit of the group. But I think it is possible.

Please don't be put off by these diverse approaches. Remember that all three agree that groups need different things at different times. Good leaders will make sure they get it—by resigning, by working with a coleader who complements their style or by changing their behavior.

The Relationship Group

The issues are quite different for a group that majors in relationships. We are social animals. We often toss our lot with others not to accomplish any specific goal but for the sheer warmth of human companionship. We sometimes need the fiction of a goal to act as a catalyst, but the real purpose of the group is fellowship. This seems to be the case for many of our church gatherings. Potluck dinners, youth fellowships, Tuesday-morning sewing circles and even prayer meetings often fall into this category. This is not to knock relationship groups. They serve a vital function.

The questions we need to deal with concerning relationship groups include:

☐ What factors create cohesiveness? What pulls people together?

☐ What can we do to foster trust and self-disclosure?

☐ How can conflict surface without tearing the fellowship apart?

☐ How can we unconditionally accept members so that they are free to be themselves?

☐ Is it possible to create a climate where an honest expression of emotion is safe?

About ten years ago I led a Bible study with high-school students who were new Christians. About fifteen guys and gals came out on an average Sunday night. The group had stability, they did their reading ahead of time, and I know they were serious about growing in the faith. Yet something was missing. There was no sparkle, no excitement, no life. We were just going through the motions.

In the middle of one listless session in Ma I shut my Bible and said, "I don't know about you, but I feel like there's a big cloud hanging over our group. I'm not sure that it's so much of a problem in our relationship with God as it is in our feelings toward each other. I'd be willing to explore this with anyone who's open to taking a look. Let's quit for tonight—we aren't getting anywhere, anyway. Next week for a one-time shot let's talk about what's going on among us. It may be a bum idea. Don't feel you have to come. But if you do, be prepared to share honestly what you're feeling about yourself and the others who are there. Is there any one who knows now that they want to be there and is willing to let us use their house?"

As a speech it wasn't very eloquent. It was filled with doubts and qualifiers. There wasn't much reaction, but one guy, Dave Plumb, volunteered his house. I showed up the next week and was surprised to find twelve there. I reiterated the rules of our meeting. Talk only about how you're feeling about yourself or others who are here. No fair bringing up folks on the outside. Try to listen with the love of Christ, tasting what another is saying before you respond. We sang a song or two and then opened the floor.

Silence. After about two minutes one girl haltingly said that she felt like a phony because she prayed with the others on Sunday night but had little contact with them in school. As openness and honesty goes, it was pretty general, but it broke the ice for others to come in. About the third guy who spoke said that he admired me and sensed that I liked him, yet he wasn't sure. I affirmed that he was a favorite of mine. Right then another fellow jumped up and said accusingly, "That's it, Em! You play favorites." Then he settled back and in a low voice added, "I'm

"I'm sorry, but we cannot complete your call as dialed. Please check the number and dial again or ask yourself if talking to someone is what you really need, or if your needs could be more readily satisfied with a better understanding of yourself and the world we live in."

not one of them, . . . and I want to be." Talk about deep emotions! I went over and hugged him. The floodgates opened. Everyone had some hurt to share or relationship to mend. Three hours later we sang another song. "We are one in the Spirit . . . ," we began, and for the first time it felt like the truth.

This kind of sharing can't take place in a vacuum. The next week some students I didn't know came up to me and said they'd heard about the fantastic night at Plumb's. In fact, the phrase "the night at Plumb's" came to symbolize much of the excitement and love that was felt within the group the following months. I hadn't planned on meeting during the summer, but they insisted. By fall the number of Christians had grown to fifty. The closeness was contagious. It was a mini-Acts 4. One of the guys told me the group wanted to have a retreat centered on prayer. I asked him what else they wanted to do. "Just pray," he said. So we did.

All this was not without problems. They didn't always have the maturity to deal with the emotions that were unleashed by this fellowship. When I got home that first night, I was on the phone with nine of the students I had just left. They had never experienced the power of such openness and decided to cut school the next day and head for the Lake Michigan dunes to continue the sharing. I had to splash cold water on that plan. I tried to explain that life goes on as usual and that the key indicator of whether or not any lasting change had occurred was how they treated each other in school. I also had to reassure some parents who were naturally concerned about what was happening to their son or daughter. And once or twice a group member got hurt by unthinking comments.

Despite these problems, the night at Plumb's remains a model of a good relational group. First, all of us knew what we were getting into. No one had to come. In fact some stayed away. The kind of vulnerability that is the mark of a good sharing group can't be forced. I've led a number of Koinonia groups since the night at Plumb's and have pulled together a set of ground rules for participants to consider.[6] None of them are original with me, but then I'm not sure the Lord gives extra credit for originality. In the secular world this is called the group's contract. That's a bit cold and legal for me. I prefer the term *covenant* which acknowledges our desire to be loving to the others because God first loved us. Whatever we call the agreement, it's important that folks who join have some idea up front what will take place. Here's what I suggest:

1. *Attendance:* I need everyone in the group in order to grow. One person's absence will affect the whole group. I will try to leave the pressures and baggage of life outside the room. For the

time I am here I will concentrate on what I am feeling at the moment and on my response to others in the group. Dealing with the stories or problems of those who are not here is helpful neither to them or us. I will stay in the here and now.

2. *Affirmation:* There is nothing you have done or will do that will make me stop loving you. I may not agree with your actions, but I will love you unconditionally. It is more blessed to care than to cure. This is not a therapy group. I will avoid the tendency to fix people.

3. *Confidentiality:* What's said here stays here! A permissive atmosphere flourishes when others are trustworthy. I will never repeat what another has said unless given specific permission.

4. *Openness:* I will strive to reveal who I am—my hopes, hurts, backgrounds, joys and struggles—as well as I am able. I'll share a story not a sermon. I can help others more by risking to be known and telling what is real to me than when I repeat a teaching I heard from someone else.

5. *Honesty:* I will try to mirror back what I see others saying and doing. This way I will help you understand something you may want to change but were unaware of. You can help me in the same way. This may strain our relationship, but I will have confidence in your ability to hear the truth in love. I will try to express this honesty, to meter it, according to what I perceive the circumstances to be.

6. *Sensitivity:* I will try to put myself in your shoes and understand what it is like to be you. I will try to hear you, see you and feel where you are, to draw you out of the pit of discouragement or withdrawal. But I recognize that you have the individual right to remain silent. Groups don't have rights; individuals do.

7. *Accountability:* I am responsible for my own growth. I won't blame others for my feelings. None of us are trapped into behaviors that are unchangeable. I am accountable to myself, others and God to become what God has designed me to be in his loving creation. I will help you become what you can be.

8. *Prayer:* During the course of this group, I will pray for the

36

other members and bask in the confidence that they are praying for me.

A second feature of a good relational group is the nature of the comments that are made by members to each other. Talk in a task-centered group focuses on the job at hand, not on members of the group. There's nothing wrong with this; in fact, working at a common task can draw us together. But talking about relationships is not part of the agenda of a task group, so it often doesn't get done. Even some so-called fellowship groups fall into this trap. They discuss God, but he's treated as a topic out there rather than as one who affects me personally. A helpful sharing group will talk about things going on inside the circle of members. Statements about the group itself are good starting points:

"I see us as a loving group."

"Do you think we're ducking our responsibility to pray for each other?"

Disclosing personal feelings or telling our story is better:

"I feel left out."

"When I hugged my dad that night, I realized for the first time that I'm a giving person."

Sharing reactions to others in the group is the best:

"Arlene, I love you."

"Pete, I get the impression you're feeling jealous of me."

This final category takes guts. Any attempt to force people to state their reactions is misguided if not downright harmful. A group can't start at this level. It takes time to build up the trust level to the point where a direct I-Thou statement is reasonable. But it only takes one or two such honest revelations to draw a disparate—and even desperate—collection of individuals into a close-knit unity. Unfortunately, many organizations that name the name of Jesus Christ never take the plunge. They shut themselves off from a "night at Plumb's."

How we say something is just as important as what we say. A third mark of healthy relational communication is that there's an element of risk in the way things are put. By *risk* I mean a person's openness to change. There's not much risk in how we usually say things. Take a typical way of expressing anger: "I guess most people feel ticked when criticized." It's ambiguous. Is he angry or not? You can't tell. And if he is irritated, is he willing to let go of it, or does he enjoy bearing a grudge? Often we confuse our meaning even more by tossing in a chuckle or laugh at the end of the sentence. That way if someone takes offense, we can say we were just joking. No risk.

A no-nonsense statement of fact is probably more honest: "You make me mad." It leaves no doubt where you stand. But there's still very little risk involved. True, you run the chance of getting a punch in the nose, but there's no hint of vulnerability —openness to change. A thus-sayeth-the-Lord type of declaration has stifled a number of Bible studies. When every pronouncement has the mood and manner of absolute truth, there's little room for movement.

How different this sounds: "Do I come across as angry right now?" The speaker is speculating. He's open to feedback. What he hears is going to affect his actions. That's risky, and it is a beneficial contribution in a group seeking closeness.

Still, you don't know for sure what he's feeling. It's possible to state your reaction in an unambiguous way and yet show a willingness to change. I call that straight talk. "It seems to me that we both want the group's attention, Bill. Is that right?" Note that the person isn't hiding his desire or perceptions. Yet there's a certain tentativeness in this kind of conversation. It's an attitude that says, "This is where I am, but I'm willing to move." It can generate great trust.

Some people get edgy with such group introspection. They feel that all this talk about feelings paralyzes—paralysis by analysis. There's no question that it can raise tension. We're asking members to be participant-observers. They need unself-consciously to throw themselves into the group process while at the same time step back and be a Goodyear blimp monitoring their own behavior. They can get bent out of shape with the dual role unless they are committed to its value. As you can probably tell, I am.

The leaders of good relational groups have to be careful not to lead too much. They aren't trying to engineer openness, merely create the opportunity for those who want it. There's also the matter of clout. Just because they lead, their words will be given extra weight. One woman I've worked with uses this standard: "Whenever I'm tempted to intervene, to help the group along, I wait a minute. Usually I find that my comment wasn't necessary. If it is, there's still time."

So the relational leader is best seen as slightly laid back, giving others the space to come into the discussion if they desire. This doesn't mean being cold or aloof. Far from it. If the head honcho models a warmth, an openness, an acceptance, others will follow suit. Leadership by example is the name of the game in relational communication.

The Influence Group

The influence group is of particular interest to Christians. It is composed of people who admit the need for change in their lives. They voluntarily gather and request that others exhort them and have an impact on their behavior and attitudes. Alcoholics Anonymous, Smoke Enders and Weight Watchers are three organizations dedicated to the abandonment of alcohol, cigarettes or food. Exercise classes and assertiveness-training sessions encourage more of something rather than less. In the Christian community, prayer fellowships and share-your-faith seminars exist to increase meditation and witness.

All of these groups can go under the general umbrella of consciousness raising. The purpose of the group is to take the thoughts and desires that lie dormant within a person and raise them to a heightened awareness. It's like fanning a glowing ember until it breaks into flame. As members become conscious of the depth of their desires, they are emboldened to stop smoking cold turkey, jog farther and faster, tell others about Jesus or do whatever action is the reason for the group's existence.

In no case, however, is it enough just to have a leader who wants to persuade others. There must ultimately be a shared desire for change on the part of the membership.

I've led a discussion group at my church on how to share your faith. By attending, most participants were tacitly saying that they were unhappy with the extent of their Christian witness. Our time together didn't consist so much of describing techniques of personal evangelism as it did of mutual encouragement and commitment to be more bold in the future. Discipleship classes and individual or group pastoral counseling often fall into this persuasive category. Some questions to ask about influence groups are:

☐ What happens when a member breaks a group's norms?

☐ How do leaders' expectations affect a member's behavior?

☐ How can they motivate the troops?

☐ What type of influence lasts the longest?

☐ Do some members in the group have more power than others?

☐ What kind of rewards can overcome the cost of change?

Right now I'm part of a loose association of men who are trying to come to grips with our use of money. It's not like we don't know what God wants. The Scripture is plain that excess funds are to be used for brethren who are hurting. (See Lk 3:10-11 and 2 Cor 8:1-15.) But we need the mutual encouragement and challenge of each other's lives to get us off the dime. We're discovering the truth that Kurt Lewin, the father of Group Dynamics, stated many years ago. "It is usually easier to change individuals formed into a group than to change any one of them separately."[8]

How come? The secret lies in mutual public commitment. Once I've told others that I'll do something, there's a loss of face if I don't. Besides that, I'd feel like I let the team down. They're struggling just as hard as I am. We've all vowed that we can do it. I have a responsibility to hold up my end of the bargain.

I'm experiencing that positive interpersonal pressure even as I

write. As a reluctant author, I can identify with the Irish poet who said:
Genius is a myth.
I get four lines to a fifth.
I don't relate to the alcoholic part, but the allusion to the agony of taking pen in hand touches a responsive chord. My version is:
Genius is a joke.
I get three lines to a Coke.
The average chapter in this book has come in fits and starts over a period of months. (Despite the fact that this one is placed early in the book, it's one of the last to be written.) Yet I'm finishing the whole thing in three days. I've made a pact with a close friend to squirrel myself away and do nothing but write until it's done. Every time I'm tempted to take a nap, watch TV or pick up the phone, I think of our commitment to each other and turn back to the page.

The influence group is successful when it has impact on the lives of the members. Things happen. A standard rule of thumb for volunteer organizations is that eighty per cent of the resources come from twenty per cent of the people. This is true whether we're talking about time, money, expertise or energy. The effective consciousness-raising group is preparing a batch of twenty percenters. All this may not be comfortable to those who are in the process of change. But as the saying goes: no pain, no gain.

Those on the outside looking in may feel threatened too. They've learned to deal with folks as they were, not with what they're becoming. They often feel an implied pressure to get caught up in the same activity. Recent converts to jogging, feminism, charismatic experiences, right to life or anything are not always high on the interpersonal sensitivity scale. But the emotion which may be scary to members and nonmembers alike is a necessary part of movement. Note the similarity of the words: emotion—motion. Strong feeling is the force that moves us to action.

What does the effective influence group look like? Picture the

41

leader as having the same characteristics as the membership—only more so! Do they walk a picket line? He's more militant than they. Is the group committed to a simple life? He'll wear jeans, a sweatshirt and eat yucca roots. Do members want to stir each other up to acts of human kindness? The leader will be a Mother Teresa of charity. None of this is said in derision. To be effective change agents, leaders must model the life their followers seek. Yet there's more to it than that.

Anyone committed to bringing about change must be comfortable with the use of power. Power has gotten a bum rap over the years. Almost any schoolboy can quote Lord Acton's famous statement: "Power tends to corrupt. Absolute power tends to corrupt absolutely." And certainly there are many examples of men and women who are power brokers selfishly wielding their influence to meet their own needs. But true leaders can use power to meet the needs of their people. They can even do better than that. They can transform their people so that they seek to serve higher needs. Thus true influential leaders ask for sacrifices from their followers rather than promising goodies. There aren't many of this breed around, but that's what good change agents are about. They empower people to live up to their potential.

Three in One

So we see that group experiences can provide three distinct services: task, relationship and influence. This knowledge won't make us more effective with people, however, unless we recognize another fact of group life. It is that individuals differ in the amount they need and desire these three separate activities.

Psychologists identify three social drives in human beings: need for achievement, need for affiliation, need for power. These match up nicely with the three types of groups I've presented. The parallels have obvious implications. Those high in need for achievement will work well in a group that has a task to do. But if they are low on need for affiliation, they may be frustrated at the seeming aimlessness of a group focusing on relationships. Members with a significant need for power may take a facilitating role in a group who's goal is influence, but unless their need for achievement is also high, their drive to have their particular solution accepted can sabotage a task group. Relationship-oriented people may blossom in a sharing group, but their high need for affiliation could cause them to hide dissenting views.

At this point we mustn't fall into the trap of assuming that one of the three motivations is more noble or Christian than another. Drive for achievement can spur us on to use our talents for the kingdom of God, or we can pursue our own selfish goals. High need for affiliation can break out into beautiful sensitivity to other people's needs, or it can foster a clinging parasitic dependency. The shakers and movers among us can use their power to further the cause of Christ, or they can be concerned only with their own personal ambition and reputation. Drives for achievement, affiliation and power are neither good nor bad in and of themselves. Moral judgment depends on how they are harnessed.

How can we spot whether another person is task, relationship or influence oriented? For that matter, how can we determine our own inclinations along this line? See which of the following descriptions best fits you or the group member in question. Or if you want to have some fun and gain insight at the same time, have a few friends tell you which paragraph most effectively captures who you are.

/ Task: I am a goal-oriented person. It's important to me to complete a job I've started. For that reason I try not to waste time. I have a strong desire to do things better, to constantly improve my performance.

/ Relationship: I am a role-oriented person. I'm very aware of what others are feeling and have strong emotional responses myself. It's important to me that people get along harmoniously. I have a strong desire to be with and enjoy other people. I don't want to be left out.

OCCUPANCY BY MORE THAN ONE PERSON IS DANGEROUS AND UNLAWFUL

| Influence: I am an effect-oriented person. I want to change the world. I'm not sidetracked by petty circumstances in my quest to have an impact on people around me. I have a strong desire to use my abilities to persuade others.

Is it possible that more than one of these descriptions might fit you? Yes. I've known quite a few people who are equally high in two of the areas. I've even spotted a few individuals who are driven hard by all three—and *driven* is the word. But most folks can point to one dominant need at work. It's also possible that you might run across some who don't feel the force of any of these needs. It's not likely that you'll meet them in a group, however. With none of these drives goading them toward social contact, they'll probably be loners.

As Christian leaders, what do we do with this information? If we have the mind of Christ, our direction seems plain. We serve! Instead of going into a group simply to meet our own needs, we must be sensitive as to why other people are present. We've got to be careful not to let our own wants dictate the group's agenda. They've come for a specific reason, and it may not be the same reason that prompts us. That's O.K. Once we're aware of their basic wants and needs, it makes sense to take some pains to meet them. In other words, scratch where they itch.

Will your group accomplish a task, build relationships or influence behavior? It's not an either/or question. All three go into every group. Rather it's a matter of emphasis.

A long view will help us be sympathetic to motivations that differ from ours. If we're seeking to accomplish a task, we need to realize that the goal will be better served if we take time to let relationship-minded people do some fence mending and let those concerned with power have significant input. If our aim is closer relationships, we must accept the fact that fellowship often comes as a by-product of cooperative work, and that a feeling of powerlessness can cut off a person from the group. If our purpose is to be a change agent, we should recognize that people are only freed to alter their style of life when the

45

change is consistent with their goals and is supported by close friends.

I quoted some rather nasty sentiments about groups at the start of this chapter. But meetings don't have to be lousy. The chances of leading a winner pick up fast when we try to attune ourselves to people's needs.

In the next chapter we will look at how people become leaders. Then the bulk of the book is divided into three sections that deal with meeting the needs for task achievement, the drive for affiliation and the desire to influence others.

Cartoon by Robert Day courtesy of Sports Illustrated Copyright © 1955 Time, Inc.

3

Take Me
to Your
Leader

It's fun for me to try to picture the person who's reading this book. First and foremost it's a book about groups and what makes them tick. So there's lots of advice on helping people work together. And since I'm a Christian, most of the examples are drawn from groups that have formed because of a common faith in Jesus Christ. What sort of person is apt to read these words?

The answer seems obvious: a Christian leader or at least someone who'd like to be. Is this you? If so, what are the chances that I can draw a mental profile of who you are? Some would figure you to be a tall square-jawed young man with a flinty gleam in your eye. But of course it's quite possible that you're a woman. Perhaps you're rising to the top by possessing the ambition of a self-starter, the kind of person that overcomes obstacles that hinder lesser mortals. Or maybe your secret of success is an outgoing, cheerful personality. Would it be silly to expect you to emit an aura of unmistakable spirituality that would cause others to raise you to a position of leadership? It's possible that you're a chain-of-command type who's found the key to effectiveness in the proper use of authority.

All of these notions may strike you as a bit simplistic. I agree. They're stereotypes. You probably don't recognize yourself in any of these descriptions. But they reflect our desire to somehow get a handle on the slippery concept of leadership. A few years ago there was a series of flying-saucer jokes. They start out with the landing of the spaceship, the hatch popping open and a little green Martian stepping out. "Take me to your leader," he'd say, and the joke went on from there. I've always been lousy at remembering punch lines, but the image of the tiny green man trying to identify who's really in charge sticks in my mind. It's a legitimate quest.

"Kindly take us to your President!"

We've begun to get a handle on what groups are and do—they get a job done, they build relationships, they change us. Before looking further into each of these topics in parts two, three and four of this book, let's consider what leaders are and do more closely.

I've had the rare opportunity to observe the fascinating process of leadership emergence these last ten years. Each summer I've taken eight different Wheaton College students to a remote island in Lake Michigan for a two-week course in group dynamics. No one is there but us. The group is responsible to plan, organize and carry out whatever happens. Transportation, cooking, cleaning the house, rules and regulations, recreation—everything but the actual course work and instruction is left up to the group. It's a set-up that fairly screams for effective leadership. Without someone taking charge, chaos reigns.

The term *taking charge* is a bit misleading. Many group members tried to assume leadership, but were rebuffed by the rest. The would-be leader assumed he had the group with him, boldly cried, "Follow me," and stepped to the fore. Looking back, however, he discovered no one was following. The term *receiving charge* better describes what actually happened. Leaders emerged slowly and only with permission of the group. Please understand that there was never any formal vote which propelled a person into a leadership position. It happened gradually until almost all recognized that there was a de facto head of the group.

Although the process of leadership emergence was roughly the same every year, the reasons why a particular member was selected were different. I've selected four specific years and have tried to capture the uniqueness of what went on with the following labels.

The year of personality.

The year of circumstances.

The year of style.

The year of service.

Each year illustrates a different approach to the study of leadership. Put the four years together and you've got a pretty clear picture of the state of the art—a best guess at what makes an effective leader.

Personality

Jim's an impressive guy. He's definitely smart. During the two-week course he took tests, solved word problems, discussed world history and played chess with equal ease. He managed to do all of this without seeming to be an egghead. He's not the typical jock, but Jim handles himself with agility on the football field and tennis court. He's fiercely competitive. Girls are attracted to his Robert Redford good looks and his unself-conscious friendly banter. He has a delightful sense of humor with the grace to laugh at himself more often than at others. He heads up one of the best Youth for Christ clubs I've ever seen. If I had to describe Jim in one word I'd say he's a participator. He throws himself into everything from a game of darts, to his course work, to a Bible study fellowship. Jim's dream is to be a U.S. Senator. I don't know of anyone willing to bet he won't make it.

When Jim signed up for the course I automatically assumed he'd become the leader of the group, and I was right. This is a clear case of the personality approach to leadership. It suggests that there are certain characteristics which will make a person a leader. Researchers who are committed to this approach will survey the personality traits of successful leaders in an attempt to find the magic formula or combination that will guarantee a person the top slot. It seems like a great idea, but unfortunately it doesn't work.[1] The search for a common thread has come up ashes. While the traits I mentioned in Jim's case are often cited as leadership qualities, there are many people with these traits who can't scare up a following. I've had at least two other people with personality credentials as good as Jim's or better who were passed over by their groups.

The best that can be said is that some characteristics will eliminate a person from consideration as leader. Friendliness

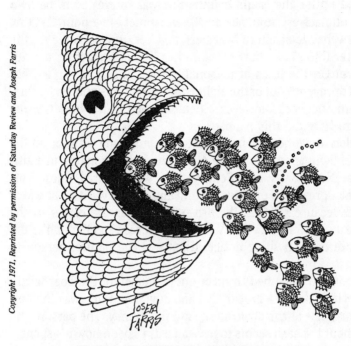

Copyright 1971. Reprinted by permission of Saturday Review and Joseph Farris

"Quit complaining! He's the only leader we've got!"

won't make you a leader, but open sarcasm and hostility will disqualify you. Active participation doesn't guarantee selection, but aloof disinterest counts you out. Ability isn't an automatic ticket to power, but you forfeit the chance to ride if you're a complete klutz.

The dead-end nature of the personality search has led some investigators to favor a situational view of leadership. They believe that circumstances can vault a nobody into the role of leader. Let's see how this might work.

Circumstances

I knew Ellen as a student in my public-speaking class before she signed up for the island course. She was interested in being a dramatic actress. But her small size (ninety-five pounds), tiny voice (I had to strain to hear her), and her unusual topic for the quarter (birds) all contributed to her lack of impact on her audience. On the basis of personality traits, I'd have ranked her sixth or seventh out of the eight contenders for island leadership. Within one week, however, Ellen emerged as the leader of the group. How did this happen?

Ellen drove her car from Boston to our jump-off spot on the Lake Michigan shore. There were course participants in Baltimore, New Jersey and Pennsylvania who wanted rides. This meant a great deal of letter writing and calling went on ahead of time. Because she was the driver, Ellen was the center of the communication network. When I was forced to change the departure date on short notice, Ellen was the natural person to contact.

The group planned to meet one hour before the boat left in order to make up a grocery list and buy food. Ellen was the first person I saw at the dock, so she got the money. The person who doles out the cash seems to have an extra say on how it's spent.

Once on the island I assigned the girls and guys sleeping quarters at random. By luck of the draw Ellen got the fold-out couch in the living room. This again placed her in the center of things. Anyone going to the washroom, kitchen or basement had to pass by. Because of her centrality in the traffic pattern, Ellen had more informal contact with the group members than anyone else.

The weather was a final contributor to Ellen's rise. Ordinarily we play long soccer games and Ellen was inept at such a vigorous sport. But the weather turned cold and rainy most of the two weeks, so we had to settle for indoor recreation. Charades was the daily fare and Ellen was a wizard at it. Her literary background and acting ability put her well above the rest of us.

All of these happenstances combined to make Ellen the acknowledged leader. The group looked to her to set the pace on cooking, household jobs, resolving conflict between members and negotiating with me on a change in course requirements. Circumstances made Ellen the leader, and she performed eagerly and well.

Style

If you've stayed with me so far, you've probably become convinced that neither personality nor circumstances tells the whole leadership story. Leadership is dynamic. Men and women can change their behavior, alter their style of dealing with other people. The style of interaction can affect who will be accepted as leader and how well he or she leads. Consider the wide range of action in the following catalog of leadership styles.[2]

Authoritarian: Authoritarian leaders make decisions for the group. Armed with superior knowledge, experience or power, they unilaterally choose what they think is best for the members of the organization. ("Father knows best.") Once a decision is made, they give the troops the word and tolerate no back talk. ("Don't confuse me with the facts; my mind's made up.") Those who adopt this "tell" style aren't necessarily harsh or uncaring. They could be benevolent dictators. It's also true that many Christians feel quite comfortable with an autocratic style. They place a high priority on terms like *chain of command, authority, discipline* and *obedience*. The danger, of course, is that the leaders and their followers will automatically assume that the leaders have a direct pipeline to God and that all of their decisions have a divine stamp of approval. ("My way is Yahweh.")

Persuasive: Persuasive leaders also have the final say-so. In fact, they often make decisions long before they check with their followers. But they are quite concerned that members back their judgment. When it comes to carrying out their ideas, persuasive leaders know that enthusiastic support is much better than grudging obedience. For this reason they work hard to sell their people on the soundness of their direction and the benefits the group will receive. This means that the influence style works best when the leader is an attractive, winsome people person loaded with charisma.

Consulting: Some pastors, managers and chairmen are more tentative in their decision making. They reserve the right to make the ultimate judgment, but they want to get all the input they can muster from others ahead of time. They probe, test and float trial balloons. Authoritarian and persuasive leaders place an emphasis on downward communication, but consulting leaders stress the upward variety. They listen more than they talk. This can foster a spirit of participation and cooperation in the group while helping the leaders get quality information on which to act. Often this style leaves leaders less tense about disagreement and criticism from below. Since the leaders' ideas are flexible and open to change until the final moment of decision, they can afford to welcome open and honest feedback.

Democratic: This style assumes that everybody involved should have a say in decisions that affect them. Leaders who go the democratic route have enough confidence in the entire group that they are willing to risk sharing their authority with them. They join with the group to consider all possible options.

Drawing by Ross; © 1981, The New Yorker Magazine, Inc.

"What I like about him is he never tells you to stay in line, he asks you to stay in line."

Their role is to guide a fair and orderly discussion that entertains all viewpoints. It's possible that the group may make what the leader thinks is a lousy decision, but he's committed to the notion that in the long run the group will best be served through a democratic process. This style requires faith in others and a good supply of Alka-Seltzer.

Laissez-faire: This is a French term meaning "to leave alone." Some leaders, though not many, subscribe to the maxim that the leader who leads least leads best. Their style isn't based on laziness or lack of concern. They truly believe that the best service they can render members is to get out of their hair so they can get on about their business. This approach can work well when everyone is knowledgeable, motivated and content. The danger is, of course, that such a rudderless ship can quickly spawn anarchy or apathy.

I've given a brief rundown on five different styles of leadership. Note that I started with an authoritarian style which places all power in the leader and allows none for the group. I then worked toward the other end of the spectrum, ending with a laissez-faire style. This abandons any claim to power and tosses all responsibility on others. Which style is best? Let's draw on my island experience again.

One year a fellow tried to direct the group with an authoritarian style. He was a championship debater, intelligent, forceful and articulate. He knew just what should be done and how to do it. His ideas were really quite good, but the others rejected his attempt to lead. They weren't about to let someone else dictate their actions. Chaos reigned until Bill stepped in with a democratic approach. Without trying to foist his own opinions onto the group, he led them through a series of decisions that got things running smoothly. People responded to Bill's low-key permissive manner.

Before you conclude that the democratic style is the way to go, remember that college students are particularly edgy about someone trying to restrict their newfound freedom—especially when that someone is a fellow student. The autocratic style bombed on the island, but it might get better results for a football coach. The laissez-faire attitude would be disastrous in running a church stewardship campaign, but the lack of interference it implies might be the best route for a college dean to follow in dealing with a productive teaching faculty. This is precisely the problem with the style approach to leadership. Just as we saw with character that there's no such thing as "a man for all seasons," we now see that there's also no one style that works best in all situations. The amount of power leaders can actually wield depends a great deal on what group members want and expect. To put it bluntly: what style will others let leaders get away with?

Service

Last winter I spoke at a three-day ski camp sponsored by a church youth group. After the first day of skiing one of the counselors pulled me aside and bemoaned, "I wish we didn't have to spend so much time on the hill. *That's* not why we're here." I had to laugh. It was precisely the reason kids had saved up sixty dollars. They'd come to ski. Contrast this leader's attitude with another counselor who was disappointed when the ski lift shut down. "With one hour more I think I could have built up Sue's confidence enough so she'd try the big slope. She wants to get out of the 'bunny bowl' so badly." Which counselor was the leader?

This story illustrates a fourth approach to leadership—service. It suggests that the real leader is the person who has the will and the skill to meet the needs of the group. These high-school students had a strong desire to feel competent on the ski hill. Anyone who helped them reach that goal would be in a position to lead.

Jesus seems to have viewed leadership in this light. "Whoever would be great among you must be your servant, and whoever would be first among you must be slave of all. For the Son of man also came not to be served but to serve, and to give his life as a ransom for many" (Mk 10:43-45).

Service to the group explains the leadership pattern on the island the fourth year. There were two leaders: Glenn and Joan. Glenn wasn't afraid of hard work. He studied diligently and helped others understand the tougher course material. When there was a job to be done, Glenn was the first one with a broom in his hand. If it was his turn to fix dinner, he took extra pains to make the table attractive and serve the food hot. He earned the right to set the pace.

Joan's leadership was of a different kind. She was a warm person and was sensitive to others' feelings. She was quick to spot the times when another member felt rejected or out of sorts. She provided a sympathetic ear for those who hurt, and she was first with a humorous quip when the group was in the mood to joke around. As Scripture suggests, Joan laughed with those who rejoiced and wept with those who cried.

Joan and Glenn were both leaders, but they served very different needs. Glenn was a task leader. His function was to help the members accomplish their goals, get the job done, further group output. Joan was a relationship leader. Her function was to hold the group together, tend to the social and emotional needs of group members, tear down fences and build bridges between folks. Note that this is the same pattern that Jessie and I adopted with the food co-op mentioned in the introduction. It worked beautifully in Glenn and Joan's case. The group allowed two service-oriented people to colead, each meeting different needs.

One caution is in order. It's been my experience that we tend to underestimate the relationship needs of people working together. We often dash blindly ahead with the job at hand, blithely assuming that everybody's happy and content. Yet underneath the calm surface, people may be seething with jealousy, hurting from rejection or just plain bored because they aren't getting human warmth. This can be especially true in Christian groups where everybody is a volunteer. No one has to stay. If the social and emotional needs aren't monitored, the group will quickly disintegrate.

Is there any foolproof way to spot servant-leaders ahead of time? No. But we can get a fairly strong indication by looking at their previous track record. If they've met the needs of people in one group, they're likely to be effective in other situations. I found this true for all of the island leaders mentioned in this chapter. All had shown a willingness to serve elsewhere. This should have tipped me off that they'd lead at the island—for if

"I've got nothing against anarchy, just as long as I am the anarch."

anything is certain in the study of leadership, it's that no one becomes a leader if he or she doesn't want it. I've never seen a genuine leadership draft or heard of a person being dragged, kicking and screaming, into office.

As Christians, we have to be careful of false humility. There's nothing immoral, illegal or fattening about the desire to lead. Paul states it bluntly. "It is quite true to say that a man who sets his heart on holding office has a laudable ambition" (1 Tim 3:1 Phillips). True servant-leaders will pay a great price in loneliness, rejection, fatigue and disappointment for the satisfaction of helping the group meet its goals. We don't need to add to the cost of leadership by making them into a hypocrite—insisting that they pretend they don't want the position.

In this chapter I've presented four approaches to leadership. I believe that personality, circumstances and style are valid clues in predicting who will lead. But for me the most helpful approach is to view leadership as service to the needs of individual members and to the cause of the group.

By now you may be tired of reading the word "needs." That kind of talk can be tiresome. But call them what you will—needs, drives, orientations, desires, motives or whatever—they are the key to effective servant leadership. To state it bluntly: *He who meets needs, leads.*

Part Two

Tasks
in
Groups

4

Methods of Decision Making

You're the chairman of the church's missions committee. You've held the post for two years and have one more year to go in your term of office. Up to now the group's duties have been routine: recruiting speakers, corresponding with missionaries, handling the funds that go to the denomination's mission board. But now you're faced with a larger responsibility. This year marks the fiftieth anniversary of your church's founding. Your pastor fears that the planned celebration will cause people to turn in upon themselves. He has a vision that the church is capable of raising $50,000 for a special missions project. He's committed to making the campaign go, but he doesn't know what the project should be. That's your job.

You aren't completely in the dark. He's given you some overall guidelines. You're to focus in on a single ministry. The church is tired of nickel and diming a hundred different agencies. Members would rather have a strong impact on one area than a fleeting brush with many. You also have a mandate to invest in people rather than things. There's nothing wrong with bricks and mortar. Capital expenditures for land, buildings and machinery enable missionaries to do their jobs. But those are relatively easy dollars to raise. The church wants to put its money into warm human beings. And of course it has to be a project that will turn people on. You're asking folks for megabucks.

There's no dearth of ideas. People can always think of ways to spend money. Already requests have surfaced and been sent to your committee for consideration. They are:

1. Support a young couple in radio evangelism. The daughter of a long-term member has recently married a Russian defector. He's been offered the chance to broadcast to people behind the Iron Curtain, but because of his background, he doesn't have the traditional support required by a faith mission. The $50,000 would cover the first three years of his ministry.

2. Use the funds to recruit indigenous doctors at a mission hospital in Bangladesh. The missionary doctor is hopelessly overworked. He's in contact with three national physicians who desire to serve God at the clinic. They're willing to take the drastic cut in pay for themselves, but don't want to penalize their children by denying them an education. The $50,000 could set up an endowment fund for the schooling of the three doctors' children.

3. One of the big problems of the church among Native Americans is a lack of a trained pastorate. Your denomination has set up a fledgling seminary that shows great promise, but its very existence is threatened by lack of funds. Your money could float the school for another year until other churches catch the vision for training Indian pastors.

4. A number of your young people have been positively affected by Young Life and Youth for Christ. These organizations have developed a joint proposal for outreach among the unchurched teen-agers of your community. Your funds would be

"It's a special model for committees ... it comes equipped with one gas pedal, 4 steering wheels and 10 sets of brakes."

seed money to launch this campaign.

5. Some of your members take seriously God's special concern for the poor. People on the island of Haiti are the poorest of the poor. Your dollars would be just a drop in a bucket if used for direct relief. But a self-help development project is another thing. You could finance a local cannery which would provide employment and keep the single crop harvest from spoiling.

6. Although your church is in a white-collar suburb, the majority of your people commute to the city for their jobs. Up to this point you've not been in touch with the problems faced by the urban church. An inner-city pastor has approached you for help in setting up a holistic ministry in a housing project. His plans include a food co-op, tutoring, legal aid, parenting classes and discipleship groups.

You and your seven-member committee are overwhelmed by the possibilities. How do you decide? That's what this chapter is about. You can see why it leads off the task section of the book.

Reaching a decision is the stated assignment of the group. It's their reason for being.

For starters, you obviously want God's will. One member has announced that it's God's will to support the radio evangelist. But you're not so sure. What makes him think he has a pipeline to divine truth? You could take a page out of the first chapter of Acts—pray and then draw straws. But that's the only known time in the early church when they made a decision like that. The Council of Jerusalem (Acts 15) makes it clear that a carefully considered decision was the order of the day. The problem you have is typical of many faced by Christian group leaders. You have to select which method of decision making to use.

A few pages from now I'm going to discuss four different routes to judgment. Unfortunately none of them is perfect. Each has its pluses and minuses. Not surprisingly, the strengths of one are the weaknesses of another. It's often a trade-off. As designated leader of the group, you have to figure out what it is you're looking for. You know you want to end up with a "good" decision. But how do you define good? I define it five ways. See if you agree with me.

Quality. Lots of things make for quality. I see it as being consistent with Scripture. Is it ethical? Does it correspond with truth as we know it? In the case of the missions committee decision, a high-quality decision is one that meets the criteria set by the pastor: focusing on a single ministry, investing in people and being capable of capturing the imagination of church members. And of course you want the most bang for the buck. It's frighteningly difficult to compare the value of words of life in Russia with food to live in Haiti, but that's the issue. The most impact for the kingdom is what we're striving for.

Time. "With the Lord one day is as a thousand years," says Peter (2 Pet 3:8). Sometimes it seems like church committees adopt the same time frame. That's O.K. if no one's in a hurry. Usually, however, time is a precious resource. The seven members on the committee all have jobs, families and other responsibilities. Not only is their time valuable, the people making the request need to be told whether it's go or no-go. Besides, if the group procrastinates, they'll miss a golden opportunity. They might find it harder to raise funds for a fifty-first anniversary project.

Commitment to the decision. This is a crucial factor. The group could reach a high-quality solution in record time, but it will turn out lousy if members aren't behind it. Suppose, for instance, that the final decision is to fund theological education at an Indian school in Arizona, yet none of the members have a personal stake in the project. They're the ones who have to sell it to the congregation. If they aren't enthusiastic, you might just as well shut the door of the seminary. The project will die aborning.

Attraction to the group. Esprit de corp, cohesiveness, closeness, fellowship—call it what you will—if you don't have it, you're in trouble. This isn't a one-shot committee that will disband with members never seeing each other again. They have to work together in the future. A good decision is one which leaves people liking each other.

Learning. As chairman of the missions committee you've learned a lot about the church's outreach. Chances are you know more than any one in the congregation. That's great. But you rotate off the committee next year. You need to help others to become knowledgeable, not only about missions but about the whole decision-making process. That's what leadership training is all about. Right now my college is in the throes of a leadership crisis. The president is retiring and no one has been groomed to fill the gap. Potential leaders atrophy when they don't have a chance to exercise their decision-making muscles.

So that's our goal. You want the group to reach a quality solution that all are committed to in a short amount of time while still liking each other and learning in the process! You may not be able to pull it off. But if you can't have everything, try to come as close to perfection as possible. Let's look at four different methods to see which one shows the most promise. Each of them has merits and pitfalls. I'll try to give an impartial account without putting my thumb on the scale.

Voting

Majority rule. That's the American way. The process of taking a vote is almost synonymous with democracy. Almost every club, organization, school board, and legislature in our culture conducts its business on the basis of majority rule. But there are differing options as to how you set that up. Let's see how this might work for the missions committee.

As chairman you lead a discussion on the relative merits of the six proposals. You try to be impartial, giving everyone an equal chance to voice his or her opinion. After an agreed upon period of time, you call for a vote. The project that receives four of the seven votes wins. If the first ballot totals three votes for Bangladesh doctors, two votes for the joint Young Life/Youth for Christ proposal, and one each for Soviet block radio evangelism and the Arizona seminary, the group would discard the losing projects and revote on the top two.

A majority decision could also come if the group discussion

"The count, Mr. Chairman, is six ayes and one neigh."

began to center on one of the projects—the inner-city work, for instance. One of the members could move that this be the official focus of the fund drive. At that point all of the discussion would focus on this single proposal. When a member's "call for the question" is supported by the others, you proceed to vote the idea up or down. In case of a three-to-three split among members, you as leader would cast the deciding vote.

Whichever route you take to get there, the final outcome is based on a "one man, one vote" principle that's consistent with democratic ideals. The solution has the support of over half the group. On paper that looks like a good way to do it. But in practice it's a mixed bag. Let's consider the drawbacks and advantages.

The quality of a majority-rule decision is usually better than what would be selected solely by the luck of the draw. Suppose that an all-knowing, all-powerful, beneficent ruler of the universe (God) singled out the holistic urban project as the best use of the money. The odds of hitting upon that specific solution merely by chance are one out of six. Surely your panel of reasonably intelligent men and women of good will can improve on that. To claim absolute accuracy would certainly be presumptuous. But it's not unreasonable to hope for a seventy-per-cent probability of success, and to call it a fifty-fifty shot would be pessimistic.

There are a number of reasons for predicting a good decision. The issue has been aired in the light of day. Everyone has had a chance to pump for his or her pet project while poking holes in the plans that seem inferior. It's a lot tougher to fool seven people than it is just one. Usually the collective wisdom of the group will be greater than the knowledge of any individual. As the saying goes, "Forty million Frenchmen can't be wrong." Four churchmen can, but I'd rather bet on their reasoned choice than on one picked at random.

The terminology—chance, odds, betting, stakes—could lead you to assume I see decision making akin to gambling. Not at all. It's just that anytime we're talking about reaching the best solution, we have to speak in terms of probability as opposed to certainty.

A relatively high-quality solution isn't the only plus for majority rule. It's possible to reach a final judgment within a short time span. Not all chairmen are comfortable with this feature. They'd rather talk an issue out until everyone seems happy. When the last holdout gives in they say, "Let's vote." In this case voting is a mere formality, the stamp of approval required for the minister. But the ballot process can take a decision that's dragging on and on and bring it to an abrupt conclusion. Used this way, voting is a method of conflict resolution.

Calling the question not only moves the group to a swift decision, it forces the members to make up their minds. I have a friend who has a terrible time figuring out what he thinks. Once in a spirit of pique I asked him if he had trouble being decisive. After a long pause he answered, "Yes and no." Voting cuts through the crud of ambivalence. Yea or nay. Up or down. There's no middle ground. People can abstain—decide not to decide. But even that option helps them clarify their stance.

Of course this time-saving feature can kick up lots of stubborn resistance to the winning solution. You can't expect people who have been voted down to do back bends in support of a decision they thought second best. Even members of the winning side may be less than happy with the choices they have been given. How many people do you know who have been truly excited about one of the presidential candidates in the past two decades?

Sometimes it's worse than that. People may be drastically opposed to the will of the majority, believing that they've done something stupid, harmful or even sinful. They will do everything they possibly can to shoot down the project before it even gets off the ground.

Suppose, for instance, that one person on your missions committee holds a deep-seated prejudice against Blacks and Chicanos. He sees any funds going to social services as money poured down a rat hole which was dug by a people of no ambition. "The poor you have with you always," he quotes Jesus, not realizing that this is a biblical mandate for a lifetime of good-Samaritan service. Needless to say, he'll hold back his contribution to an inner-city effort by the church. It's also not hard to imagine him working subtly to torpedo the fund-raising campaign.

Attraction to the group follows the same pattern. We think folks who see things our way are very fine fellows indeed. "My idea of an agreeable person is a person who agrees with me." So decisions by majority rule tend to draw us closer to those on our side of the issue but alienate us from those who differ. This divisive feature is tempered by having multiple chances to cast ballots on varied issues so that my opponent in one case is my ally in another. The leader can also model an attitude of concilia-

© Mary Chambers, 1981 Appeared *in* Leadership

"Good news, Reverend. The board has voted to pray for your recovery . . . the vote was 5 to 4."

71

tion and encourage the group to see the outcome as one guided by the Holy Spirit. Overall, however, voting acts as an irritant to group cohesion.

Voting and learning go hand in hand. The push and shove of parliamentary debate is a great training ground for leadership. I suppose it's possible for some to survive a number of motions, seconds, amendments, calls for tabling and calls for the question, without picking up a certain sensitivity for guiding a discussion, but they'd have to work at it! In like manner the airing of different viewpoints is a great way for everyone to become knowledgeable about the topic at hand. By the time the vote is cast, all the members of the missions committee should know a lot more than they did at the start.

So overall the scorecard on voting as a method of decision making looks something like Figure 1.

	Quality	Time	Commitment to solution	Attraction to group	Learning
Voting	+	+	+/−	−	+

Figure 1

Not bad. But the very process which makes for the three pluses seem to create uneasiness within and between some members. Maybe it's too risky having people hammer out decisions while eyeballing each other. Perhaps things would go smoother if the group appointed an expert to make the decision for them. Many groups opt for this method. Let's take a look at the pros and cons.

Appointing an Expert
This is not as easy as it first sounds. Deciding to go to an expert still entails figuring out a way to pick him or her. Of course you or the pastor could do the deed by simple fiat. But a dictatorial solution is outside the spirit of this book which is, after all, on

group leadership. A group can give its authority to a single wise person, but it can't duck the responsibility for making a good selection. And that's tough.

There's an old saw about a teacher who asked a dozing boy to define the difference between ignorance and apathy. He replied sullenly, "I don't know, and I don't care," thus earning an A. Although he had unknowingly stumbled onto the distinction, most folks have trouble separating one from the other in practice. It's easy to confuse boredom with stupidity. The converse is also true. We often confound enthusiasm with ability. When it comes to selecting a competent pro, there's rarely a lack of volunteers. Self-styled experts always come to the fore. The trouble is that the guy who wants to be appointed resident guru may not understand his own limitations. The girl who has the wisdom of Solomon may be too shy to put herself forward.

It's especially hard to pick the best member from within your midst when the possibility of hurt feelings lurks just beneath the surface. I remember a time I was counseling at a high-school summer camp. Kids were divided into four teams for sports competition. As coach of one of the teams, it was my job to sign them up for the big swim meet. We needed one swimmer for each event. "Girls' fifty-yard backstroke! Who'd like to enter?" I shouted at the team meeting. Two girls volunteered. How was I to pick between them? I asked if either of them was on a swim team. Both nodded. Did they remember their times for the fifty-yard backstroke? No. They even looked alike! The only noticeable difference was that one gal was eager to do it while the other was somewhat reticent. So I picked the former—and she drowned! Well, not literally, but almost. Later on in the week I saw the second girl swim. I had a Junior Olympics swimmer on the team that could have won the race wearing army boots! She hadn't volunteered because she'd just washed her hair and didn't want to get it wet again!

So identifying your best person is tricky. Getting him or her to volunteer their expertise is an additional hurdle to cross. As one pastor put it, "When I'm looking for a really good man, I start my search among the people who don't have time. The good ones are always busy." But even if you identify and recruit the best person in your group, you still run up smack against a barrier to getting a top-quality solution. With one person, even the best person, you can't get synergy.

You may not be familiar with the term *synergy*. (You're not alone. I once had a student define it on a test as "sufficient energy to sin.") It refers to a group solution that is better than the best idea of any one member. It doesn't always happen, but the eureka-type solution which comes about when members pool their experience can have people scratching their heads muttering, "Now why didn't I think of that before?" Selecting a single individual cuts you off from that possibility.

Delegating the judgment to one person looks much better when time is a crucial consideration. You may not get a good decision, but you can get it fast. Sometimes that's just as important. All six mission projects have their strong points. It would be a shame to fritter away the golden opportunity through indecision. Besides, six committee meetings can consume eighty-four work hours of precious time in six two-hour meetings. One quickie meeting of the committee to select the pro, plus his or her time spent in research will probably add up to only ten or fifteen hours of work.

Group members will usually go along with a decision made by someone else as long as they don't see it as central to who they are or what they are about. Should the missions brochure be printed in four colors at ACME press or in two colors by ACE printers? Who cares? Big deal! Let someone who knows the business decide. If the girl who married the Russian defector is my niece, however, or I met the Lord through the ministry of Young Life, I want some part in deciding which project we pick. Even if I agree with the decision, I won't work as hard if I wasn't involved in the process. I'll be apathetic or even hostile to an idea that hasn't been shaped by my input. So delegating the choice to an expert does little to insure member commitment to the plan of action.

It's a bit stronger on group cohesion. You'll recall that one of the drawbacks of voting was that it split the group into two opposing camps. Appointment removes that source of irritation. Members don't have to hassle over potentially divisive issues, so they're free to enjoy each other's fellowship. It's not the best-friend type of attraction that comes out of the crucible of common stress. But a warm mutual appreciation can grow while members are waiting for the final word.

Appointment is a big zilch when it comes to learning. True, the man or woman who knew something about missions is selected and now knows *more* about missions. But the rest are left out in the cold. Their ignorance confirmed, they conclude that it takes a seminary degree to decipher the nuances of missiology.

Overall, the scorecard on selecting a knowledgeable representative is not great. It looks something like Figure 2.

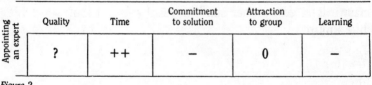

	Quality	Time	Commitment to solution	Attraction to group	Learning
Appointing an expert	?	+ +	–	0	–

Figure 2

The time required is fine and attraction to the group isn't negative. But the quality is questionable at best and commitment to the solution and learning are lacking. Isn't there a method that will offer a shot at synergy without drawbacks in involvement and cohesion? Perhaps some kind of statistical averaging technique could do the trick.

Statistical Averaging

The process I'm going to describe already has a technical name—

the Delphi technique.[1] To me that calls up images of an ancient Greek oracle making decisions by consulting the entrails of a pig. That is decidedly not what this method is about. The technique involves collecting the decisions of each member and subjecting these to a process of averaging. It's akin to combining judges' scores at a gymnastics meet or figure-skating competition. What emerges is a group decision without the need of ever calling the people together. So it's a phantom group, one in name only. The method doesn't involve sophisticated mathematics. A pocket calculator or a person with a sharp pencil and similar mind can handle the data.

As chairperson you would solicit suggestions for the anniversary project. You can do this by mail, phone or in one-on-one interviewing. Let's suppose you generate a list of the six proposals presented at the start of this chapter. You'll want to make a command decision as to whether all meet the three criteria of your original mandate. Assuming they do, you then ask committee members to rank the projects in order of their desirability. The first choice is assigned number one, and the least favored alternative is rated number six. The results might look something like Figure 3.

	You (Chrm)	Joe	Sue	Bill	Pat	Jane	Mike	Total	Place
Radio evangelism	5	1	1	4	5	5	2	23	3
Bengali doctors	3	3	5	6	3	1	1	22	2
Indian seminary	6	4	3	5	4	4	5	31	6
Youth outreach	4	5	2	1	6	3	4	25	4
Haitian cannery	1	6	6	3	2	6	3	27	5
Urban church	2	2	4	2	1	2	6	19	1

Figure 3

The next step is to present this information to the committee without identifying who voted for what. They can study the data and draw their own conclusions before you survey them a second time. If I was leader of the group, here's what I'd be thinking:

☐ No use wasting #1 choice on the cannery project. It's a dead issue. Three people are strongly opposed.

☐ Radio evangelism is right up there, but I just can't see it. Sometimes I'm more sure of what I'm against than what I'm actually for. I think I'll put it last on my list next time to try to keep it from moving up.

☐ The native American seminary doesn't stir much interest one way or the other.

☐ The group is really split on radio evangelism and education for the physician's children in Bangladesh.

☐ There's general though not unanimous support for holistic inner-city ministry.

You then ask the folks to rank the items again. They can list them exactly the same way they did the first time; or in light of the initial results, they can rearrange their priorities. It's possible to go through this cycle six or seven times, but things usually shake down after the second ranking. Given its initial edge, urban ministry would probably continue to lead the pack. But Iron Curtain broadcasting or Bengali education have a shot. The lowest total is the group's choice even though the group never actually met together.

The big advantage of statistical averaging is the equal weighting of each member's input. Statistics are no respecter of persons. The big giver, the handsome man or the woman who's clever with words can't sway the group to their side. It's truly a balanced "one man, one vote" system. Strange ideas get submerged by proposals that have general support.

I saw a perfect example of this when I once assigned different methods of decision making in my group dynamics class. I had students indicate the order in which Christ called the disciples. Note that this is a problem with a right answer, although it takes a harmony of the Gospels to ferret it out. The voting group was heavily influenced by a self-confident fellow who was a Bible major. He was certain that John was first and Philip was the last one called. But he was certainly wrong, and turned out to lead others astray. The group using the statistical averaging technique avoided the problem. There just wasn't any room for wheeling and dealing.

You'd think that any system of averaging would render a mediocre decision. Not so. The Delphi technique seems to tap into the collective wisdom of the group. Of course a computer is no better than the input it gets. That idea is reflected in the programmer's term GIGO. It stands for "Garbage in—garbage out." But my students put some good stuff in, so a superior solution came out. As long as most folks have a decent grasp of the topic at hand, the solution will be at least as good, if not better.

In terms of time, computer selection is great. It takes only a few minutes to rank a list of possible choices. One person can quickly tabulate the results. But the very efficiency of the method prevents members from drawing close to each other. There is no chance to compare ailments, swap jokes or show pictures of the new collie pup. None of these would directly help your missions group make a decision, yet they're the stuff that interpersonal attraction is made of. We can be a bit cynical by saying that as long as there's no interaction folks won't have reason to get ticked off at each other. But that's a pretty poor reason to recommend the adoption of a mechanical process.

Learning isn't much better. I may catch a glimpse of social reality by seeing how others rank the items, but there's no opportunity to discuss relative merits. It usually takes the public push and pull of ideas to stimulate new insights. Leadership training is also nonexistent. The biggest drawback of statistical averaging, however, is the total lack of member commitment to the solution.

The dean at my college was under pressure to cut back the number of academic majors. What should go? Geology, art, anthropology, Christian ed, archaeology or horror of horrors, speech communication? He sent all faculty members a list of the twenty-eight majors we offered and asked us to rank them in order of their value to a Christian liberal arts education. He computed the results and claimed the composite opinion was the faculty's decision. The reaction was instantaneous. Everyone was ticked off about something. I didn't like it because speech communication was in eighteenth place. An obvious mistake. Surely my field was in the top ten. Others questioned the integrity of the data processor. There was no sense of ownership. As one faculty member put it, "Well, that's certainly not my opinion." The dean wanted to drop the bottom three majors, yet had no faculty support. It may have been a wise solution, but I don't think there was one professor who picked those specific three fields to get the ax. Instead of fostering commitment for action, the automatic averaging merely sparked resistance.

So the print-out on statistical averaging looks like Figure 4.

	Quality	Time	Commitment to solution	Attraction to group	Learning
Statistical Averaging	+	++	--	0	-

Figure 4

Commitment to the solution has been a problem with all three methods discussed so far. Is there a technique that will guarantee member enthusiasm for the decision? Yes, there is. It's not easy to accomplish, but when it's done right, people are leaking steam to put the decision into practice. The method is called consensus.

Consensus

When I say consensus, the picture that comes to mind is the

seven members of the missions committee sitting around a table all nodding their heads in agreement sounding out their whole-hearted support. That would be great! If all the folks can coalesce on a given project, you know that the group will break their backs to make the fund drive go. When member commitment is crucial, it makes sense for the leader to take pains to insure that everybody is behind the action. But maybe you're thinking, "You're dreaming, Em. I can barely get the seven of us to agree on the divinity of Christ. No way is such a diverse group going to reach unanimity on a single plan. Even if it was possible, it'd take scads of time."

I never promised that consensus was easy. Unless your committee is acting as a rubber stamp, it can take hours of questioning and probing to reach a unanimous opinion. There's not even a guarantee you'll get it in the end. But it is possible.

Think of a twelve-member jury. That's probably the most familiar example of decision making by consensus. One person can hold up the group if he or she has a reasonable doubt. This forces the group to talk things out along the lines of evidence. The old movie *Twelve Angry Men* had Henry Fonda as the one hold-out against an eleven-man majority that wanted to rush to judgment. They were incensed at Fonda's stubbornness. But the law states that eleven to one isn't good enough. They have to reach consensus. By the end of the third reel Fonda has converted them all to a not guilty position. This may seem far-fetched, but it's been known to happen in real life.

Of course, a jury has a relatively simple task. Their decision is a simple one of yes/no, guilty/not guilty. They don't have to generate ideas to support their choice. That's up to the prosecutor and lawyer. And supposedly they are free from personal involvement with the case. None of these are true in our missions committee example. But perhaps the example of a jury shows that consensus is a possibility worth striving for when the stakes are high.

Can you reach consensus? There's no certainty. You may become a hung jury. But how the leader leads is crucial for con-

Drawing by Booth; ©1979,
The New Yorker Magazine, Inc.

BOOTH.

*"We may as well go home. It's obvious that this meeting isn't going
to settle anything."*

sensus to be reached. Sticking to the following guidelines is vital if you want to give your group a decent shot at reaching agreement.[2]

1. Announce your intentions right from the start. Let folks know that you are prepared to hash things out until the group reaches a decision that everyone can support. This means that a single person has veto power. One member can block a decision if he or she feels it's taking the group down the wrong path. Obviously this could result in total chaos if everybody pumps for their top choice. So encourage a mutual forbearance where people listen to each other's thoughts.

2. Be a process person. As leader your concern is more on how the group decides as opposed to which of the six options they pick. So be a bit suspicious of quick agreement. When you publicly check out the reason why people are in favor of a given idea, they may discover that they don't see eye to eye. Better for everybody concerned that they discover it now and wrestle

through disagreement. You want to end up with a true unity, not just a papered-over rift.

3. Encourage open expression of disagreement. Conflict isn't necessarily bad. It can be healthy. It's quite probable that some members have come to the group with hidden agendas (pet ideas that they are privately committed to). If these thoughts stay beneath the surface, they'll keep people from honestly considering other possibilities. They'll shoot down everyone else's plan, and you'll never know why. Better to get all the ideas on the table.

4. Don't mistake silence for agreement. It may seem reasonable to assume that people would speak up if they objected to the drift of the conversation. Some will. The average group has a few members that have no unspoken thoughts. They say whatever flits into their brain. But the same group will typically have one or two members who are slow to voice their opinions. They may be naturally shy. Perhaps they're intimidated by higher status or more belligerent members. They might just be slow in coming to realize what it is they do think. Whatever the reason, you need to create an environment that's supportive of their ideas. Seek out their thoughts, encourage them to plunge into the conversation.

5. Don't expect complete unanimity. That's not really your goal—which is indeed fortunate, because it's almost impossible to achieve this side of heaven. What you're shooting for is a solution that can gain everybody's approval. A lot of folks aren't sure what's best. But everybody has strong opinions about what's worst. I may not know what I'm for, but I sure know what I'm against. So your job is to help people discuss an alternative that all favor, even if it isn't first on everyone's list.

How might this look in the missions group? When I presented the vote method I speculated that you might have a prejudiced guy who would sabotage a majority decision to aid an urban congregation. The mere fact that you won't allow the group simply to outvote him may diffuse some of his opposition. Prejudice is deep-seated and tough to shake. But reasoned discussion might reveal that his main irritation with an inner-city project is that he sees dollars going to people too lazy to work. If you can craft a plan of action where the funds are used as loans to start small businesses, as seed money for youth employment and for child care for working mothers, there's a good chance he can be won over. While not an ardent fan, he'll at least give grudging support. And he may surprise you and become a booster of urban aid.

Consensus also stimulates learning. The students who had to decide the order Christ called the disciples pooled and weighed everyone's knowledge on the topic. The group as a whole came out of the session smarter than they went in. And New Testament history is just part of the gain. Sensitive observers of the human scene will have gotten a short course in group dynamics. They will be able to draw upon this interpersonal experience when they are tossed into another problem-solving situation.

There remains the question of member attraction. Does consensus make for cohesion? I know of nothing that will pull people closer together than a common commitment to unity. The Christian song "We Are One in the Spirit" is a hymn of consensus.

I once invited a class of sixteen students to our home for an informal evening together. I left the actual night and time up to them. I only asked that no one be scheduled out. Given night courses, jobs, family responsibilities, church work and travel plans, this was an almost impossible assignment. But they stuck with it. After a prolonged discussion, they finally arrived at a date which fifteen of them could make. It wasn't easy. Many of them had to flex their schedules to accommodate the group. But even so, there was one international student who was still shut out. He worked five nights a week and desperately needed the money. The two nights he was free a number of the others had unbreakable commitments. It looked like an impasse, but the group refused to quit. They entertained a number of possible solutions— some quite bizarre.

Then one girl suggested, "What if we all chip in a buck and hire someone to replace you that night. You'll still get paid, the work will get done, and we'll all be together!" Everyone chimed in their agreement. The guy looked confused. He admitted that the plan was feasible, but he couldn't believe that they'd do this for him. When the reality sank in he was ecstatic. The evening was a huge success, and I've never had a closer group of students.

Two notes of caution in all this euphoria. If the group tries to reach consensus and fails, the resulting frustration can cause interpersonal attraction to plummet. It's easy to find a scapegoat for the group's problem. Everyone blames someone else.

The opposite tendency is equally dangerous. The group may become so intent on having unity that no one can afford to raise honest doubts. This desire for togetherness-at-all-costs can lead to false consensus. The phenomenon has been labeled groupthink.[3]

Groupthink is a special danger in Christian groups that treat all disagreement as schism. That kind of atmosphere has a chilling effect on creative thinking. It's often the result of a leader who subtly promotes the view that opposition to him is sin. But closeness isn't the *aim* of consensus, rather it's the *by-product* of true agreement.

Well, by now you may be thoroughly confused as to which method of decision making to use for your missions committee. Perhaps a summary scorecard will help bring order out of chaos. I've added the pluses and minuses on consensus to those of the other three methods. The results look like Figure 5.

No method is perfect. They all have problems, but each one has something to recommend it as well. Voting is a good all-around route to go. It's familiar, it doesn't take too long, and the decision reached is usually decent. But the losers may feel grumpy and flag in zeal when it comes time to implement the decision.

Appointing an expert is one way of handling things with dispatch. By doing it you avoid squabbles between members. But then there's no guarantee the decision will be a good one. There's also no ownership of the solution.

	Quality	Time	Commitment to solution	Attraction to group	Learning
Voting	+	+	+/−	−	+
Appointing an expert	?	++	−	0	−
Statistical averaging	+	++	−−	0	−
Consensus	++	−−	++	++	+

Figure 5

Statistical analysis offers the intriguing blend of a quick, high-quality decision. But it treats the human side of decision making as nonexistent. And that's what members will be when it comes time for group effort.

Consensus promises the wisdom of Solomon together with the kind of member commitment, attraction and learning that a leader dreams of. But remember—all these people pluses come only when consensus is actually reached. If the process is abandoned, these benefits disappear. And the time involved in reaching consensus is horrendous.

So what's it going to be? It's your choice. Me? If the decision is a really big one, like a $50,000 fund-raising project, I'd opt for consensus. You could tell it was my favorite because I saved it for last. But now it's up to you.

If you do select consensus as your method to reach a decision, you'll need to draw heavily on the five guidelines I gave for leading that kind of discussion. But there are other types of discussion besides those that move toward a decision. In the next chapter we will look at how to stimulate group members to grapple with an idea and to share their reactions.

5

Leading
a
Discussion

I was one of the few Christians in my fraternity at the University of Michigan. I hit upon the idea of leading a Bible study as a way of sharing my faith with the guys in the house. As president of the local Inter-Varsity chapter, I felt an additional pressure to have a successful discussion. Not only did I care about the guys, I also wanted the Bible study to be a model of effective evangelism.

Seven fellows joined me the first night. They came for a variety of reasons. One was a philosophy major interested in batting around ideas. Another was my best friend who felt obligated to come. There was the loner who admitted he wondered what the Bible had to say, while two were openly scornful of anything smacking of religion and came out of curiosity. The final two were Christians who had prayed with me ahead of time for the venture.

I announced at the start that this would be a free and open discussion concerning God and life, kicked off each week by a passage from the Bible. Privately I was committed to using the time as a way of convincing them to believe the gospel. I was excited that so many had showed up and vowed to myself not to waste the time with idle chatter.

From that point on it was all downhill. The memory is still too painful to recount all the gruesome details, but perhaps a few examples will serve to highlight the failure.

The first night we looked at John 3. I'd prepared a series of study questions to stimulate discussion. But some were far too simplistic. (When did Nicodemus come to Jesus? According to John 3:16, what's necessary for us to inherit eternal life? When Christ talked about being born again, was he talking about physical birth?) Others required special biblical knowledge. (What was Christ referring to when he spoke of Moses lifting up the serpent in the wilderness? Who were the Pharisees?) Since I was the only one who knew the right answer I ended up lecturing on these matters. Both kinds had a chilling effect on free-wheeling dialogue. The philosopher and two scoffers never came back.

The second week I determined to give them some meat to chew on. We studied Galatians 5—the deeds of the flesh versus the fruit of the Spirit. Questions such as, "What do you think Paul means by love?" sounded pallid to me. The halting discussion was punctuated with large gaps of silence.

An hour before the third week's discussion my best friend hastily told me he had to go to the library. One of the Christian fellows was similarly occupied. People were voting with their presence—or lack of it. The other Christian and the seeker of truth struggled to respond to my questions about sin, the law and righteousness from Romans 3. At the end of the hour the loner thanked me for leading the discussion. He said that he had wanted to investigate what was in the Bible. Now he had found out enough and didn't think he'd come back. As he walked out of my room I overheard him remark to my Christian brother, "I never knew that talking about God could be so boring." No one came the following week. The great evangelistic discussion folded its tent.

It would have been easy to mutter pious complaints about the frivolous nature of my fraternity brothers or see myself as the victim of persecution that Christ predicted for those who are followers of the cross. Fortunately, I had the grace to realize that my own inept discussion skill was the cause for the exodus. I vowed that I'd learn to do it right the next time. I've since learned that lots of other leaders are in the same fix. They're good at putting out the word. But they've never had any training in the art of encouraging others to participate. With today's needed emphasis in the church on two-way communication, it's important to set it up well. It's only through dialogue that a leader will find out what the group really feels.

Why Discuss?

Before a leader even calls people together, he or she needs to honestly face the question, "Do I really want a discussion?" The answer is not an automatic yes. Many times we try to use a discussion format because it's a popular group technique. Our members want it or our superior expects it, but in our heart-of-hearts, we're uncomfortable with the loss of control. Many college professors are rotten discussion leaders because they're afraid to find out what their students are thinking. It's a threat to discover that your neatly organized lecture didn't come across clearly. My college Bible study is another example. I had a "hidden agenda." My actual purpose in calling the guys together wasn't to have a mutual interchange of ideas. I billed it as a task group—to learn. But it was really an influence group—to convince them to become Christians! They weren't dumb. They easily spotted my ulterior motive and became defensive.

Don't get me wrong. I'm all for evangelism. My book *The Mind Changers* is dedicated to the art of Christian influence.[1] In that book I set forth a three-step model of persuasion. We must first *melt* people, then *mold* them, then *make hard* their new conviction. A discussion group can be a fine place to get people questioning, doubting old beliefs, churned up over new ideas. That's melting, and it's a precondition for change.

While a discussion doesn't lend itself to direct influence, however, it is an ideal way to find out what others are thinking. There are a number of reasons leaders might seek this kind of feedback. They might be soliciting new ideas for the group. They may want some clues as to how others are responding to their leadership. Or they can use it to find out where others are. To influence others later it's necessary to discover their present attitude. Sensitive counselors at Christian camps see this as the purpose of cabin devotions. Instead of using the time as a way of delivering another message (filling in the gaps that the speaker missed), they solicit reactions to the day's events. But the leader uses the information to plan and adjust the next day's activities.

The average lecture/message/sermon is about as interesting as watching grass grow. The group member can listen much faster than the speaker can talk. So he slouches down in his chair, shifts into neutral and passively lets the speaker's words wash over him. But discussion calls for response. It takes energy to figure out what you want to say in a constantly changing discussion. The heart begins to beat; the juices begin to flow. I'll be closed to new ideas as long as I can hang back and not express my thoughts. But if you can jog me into debating the merits of my opinion, I may start churning inside. Once my rigid views are thawed I might be willing to consider a different or even "wrong" position.

A discussion group is a lousy place to mold a person's opinion. One of the classic essays on group leadership lists behaviors that contribute to a defensive climate.[2] Actions that show evaluation, control, strategy, superiority and certainty all have a chilling effect on spontaneity. Persuasion is the common thread which runs through these five behaviors. No wonder my Bible study flopped. I didn't really care what others thought. I was merely trying to maneuver them into verbal assent with my predetermined position.

So is it wise to use a discussion format for an evangelistic Bible study? To melt, yes. To mold, no. To mold usually requires a variety of influences, different settings, different people and time. If I cared about the others in the study, I would have spent time with them individually, identifying their needs, meeting them as I could and showing how God could meet them as well. As they watched me and other Christians, read the Bible and other literature, reflected on their life and opened themselves to God, and as we prayed, God would mold them. A mere discussion is inadequate to do all this.

I've found discussion a great way to solicit feedback and stimulate involvement. I've got to get it clearly in mind that I'm not trying to persuade. My aim is rather to stir up others to the point that they're willing to take the risk of saying what they think. Then I'm ready to plan a discussion.

The Place

A high energy level is the mark of a good discussion. The physical setting can either contribute to the vitality of the dialogue or it can sap the life out of the beast. Here are some tips that I've found can make a positive difference.

Meet in a room small enough to put you in touch with each other. Bank lobbies and church fellowship halls may be impressive, but the cavernous space they allow between people kills intimacy. You aren't looking for the detached contemplation distance affords. Furniture can cause trouble. Tables and overstuffed chairs can effectively block close contact. You'd gladly trade elegance for the quick response that comes from immediacy.

Seat people in a circular fashion so that everybody can see all the faces in the group. Theater-style seating is fine for focusing attention on the leader, but you don't want that. Your aim is to make each member the star. It's their reaction that counts. You're much more likely to get it when people can eyeball each other.

Make sure there's enough light. You certainly don't want the harsh brightness of a police interrogation room, but neither do you want to lull folks to sleep. The soft, low lighting of an intimate restaurant affords privacy. Dim lighting, however, doesn't give members the chance to pick up nonverbal cues. I regretfully avoid trying to lead a discussion around a flickering fire. It's cozy, but the normal tendency is to stare deeply into the fire and miss what's happening in my neighbor.

Stay indoors unless stuffiness is unbearable. My students clamor to hold class out on the lawn at the first sign of spring. I'm tempted to give in, but sad experience dictates that I resist the pressure. There are so many distractions—people walking by, the sound of a lawn mower, an ant crawling up a leg, damp grass —that the topic at hand gets lost in the shuffle. It's easy to lie back and tune out as the puff clouds march across the sky. So I stay inside. Even though I'm momentarily a dirty guy, the discussion prospers because of my resolve.

Most of these suggestions are rather obvious. You'll come up with your own check list for your situation. Just make sure that you don't lose sight of your ultimate goal. Structure the physical setting to stimulate lots of "back and forthness" between people. You'll have a winner if folks temporarily forget where they are and lose themselves in the excitement of stating their beliefs.

Building Bridges Not Walls

There's a truism in the field of communication that states: Communication = Content + Relationship.[3] Whether the goal is to persuade someone to buy life insurance, reach a joint decision or comfort a bereaved friend, two factors come into play—the words that are said and how each party feels about the other. Since words are the name of the game, it would be natural for us to focus upon the content aspect of communication. Yet we do so to our peril. No matter how provocative our discussion questions or brilliant our repartee, the dialogue will become monologue if the relationship with the leader is out of kilter. As you prepare to lead a discussion, here are some things you can do to insure that the group will *want* to participate.

Learn names. There's nothing quite as demoralizing as being referred to as "the tall man with the beard in the back row." The mere possibility makes me want to sit on any idea I might share. Yet if someone takes the care to learn my name, suddenly I'm important. I count. I want to respond.

There are all sorts of ways to remember people's names. I try to get a vivid impression of a prominent characteristic—long blond hair, a ski-jump nose, brooding dark eyes, a square jaw. Then I associate it somehow with their first name. I don't worry about last names. I have enough trouble remembering the Christian name, and that's the one that counts in an informal discussion. I try to use a person's name immediately after I hear it. "Use it or lose it" applies to name recall as much as it does to any other skill.

Of course you may be called to meet with an entirely new group. You'll probably do better to ask them to wear name tags with the first name written large. If participants are sitting at a conference-type table I bring along a stack of 5" x 8" file cards and a magic marker. One lengthwise fold makes the card prop up on the table at just the right angle so I can see the inch-high letters. The whole name-tag business may seem juvenile to some, but it's much warmer to call on people the way they like rather than pointing and saying, "Hey you."

Of course learning a name is just the first step of developing a relationship. I was asked to be the Spiritual Enrichment Week speaker at a small liberal arts college in the South. The administration was trying to rekindle a Christian emphasis on campus and the students were understandably wary of me as an outsider who was coming to lay enlightenment upon them. I tried to spend lots of time in the cafeteria, playing tennis and generally engaging in the art of small talk. I also cheered for the soccer team. At the end of the week one of the girls who spoke up the most in the discussions told me how carefully students moni-

"You want to know what we need around here? I'll tell you what we need around here. We need name tags around here."

tored this effort. "The most important thing you said all week was, 'Yea, team!' When we saw you losing your cool cheering for us we knew you were one of us. It was safe to tell you what we really thought."

Counselors at Christian camps often eat at a separate table and seem to work at setting themselves apart from the campers. Then they wonder why it's like pulling teeth to get the kids to open up when it's time to get serious. The answer is obvious. People talk openly with those they like. It's no different in a discussion.

A difference in status can kill a lively debate before it starts. My wife and I don't find it particularly helpful to be known as

Dr. and Mrs. Griffin when working with our church's junior-high program. We're comfortable being called Jeanie and Em, and the kids seem to take a certain delight that we make an effort to bridge the gap. Informal dress works to minimize the gulf. I shuck my sport coat and tie before I enter the youth lounge. It's their turf and I'll be better able to stimulate honest feedback if I blend in with the motif.

When I think of status differences I call to mind the president of my school. He's an extremely intelligent, impressive man of God. But he's got two strikes against him at the start of a discussion—precisely because of his imposing qualifications. Although he makes every effort to be evenhanded when chairing a meeting, he can't cast off the authority of his office. Under our hierarchical form of governance, he wields too much power for faculty members to feel completely at ease. Bosses, teachers, generals and ministers often face a similar problem. Any way they can divest themselves of their accumulated clout will prove helpful when they're seeking an honest reaction from their people.

Popping the Question
Up to this point my advice has been a matter of simple common sense. Posing questions that elicit response is tougher. Since it doesn't come naturally, I'll take a bit more space to outline an approach that works. Asking the right question can make or break a discussion.

The first thing I've discovered through sad experience is *don't ask a question with a right answer.* The worst offender is one that can be answered with a simple yes or no. I was working with a group of non-Christian high-school guys. I wanted to get them thinking about the divinity of Jesus. I was afraid they thought he was merely a good man. After a fun day of skiing we sat down together and I launched out, "What do you think, guys? Is Jesus Christ really God?"

I leaned forward expectantly preparing for a rousing thirty-minute discussion. No one spoke. I'm not sure they even breathed.

It was like a prayer meeting—every head bowed; every eye shut. They wouldn't look at me for fear of being called on. I restated the question, "Is Jesus really God?" After the pressure became unbearable, one bold soul took the plunge. "Yes," he said. End of discussion!

All attempts to go further fell flat. Was he really convinced of Christ's identity? "Uh-huh." How about the other guys? They all nodded their heads in mute agreement. To this day I have no idea of what they really thought about the deity of Christ.

What went wrong? I'd asked a question with a right answer. Not only that. The fellows could tell there was a right answer. Uninitiated into spiritual matters though they were, they had the street savvy to spot a loaded question. Their reasoning could go something like this: "Em's looking for something. He's been to seminary and has studied this sort of thing. I'm almost positive the answer is yes. If I say it and I'm right, I'll get his approval. But my buddies will think I'm 'brown nosing.' And suppose it's a trick question and I'm wrong? Then Em will put me down, and I'll feel like a fool before my friends. It's safer to just keep quiet." So they did. As they saw it, they were in a no-win situation.

Is it possible to have a Christian discussion without asking questions of truth? Yes. Suppose you want to stimulate thinking about the Sermon on the Mount. The typical format would include questions such as: What are the different components of the Lord's Prayer? How did Jesus enlarge the commandment about adultery? What is the Lord's attitude toward seeking riches? All of these are questions of fact, and they are almost guaranteed to generate little reaction.

On the other hand you could ask: "You've read the Sermon on the Mount. Suppose Christian kids in your school were able to put its teachings into effect for just one week. How would things be different?" That's a whole different ball game. Instead of one right answer there are lots of possibilities. No one of them is right. Joan can think that non-Christians would be threatened while Bill might conclude that it would be heaven on earth.

There's room for disagreement, even an argument. And since there's no way you can authoritatively state that they are wrong, neither of them fear being shot down by the leader. This suggests the second principle of popping the question.

Make them the experts. I was a counselor at a Young Life weekend camp. Although it was past midnight, the twelve guys in my cabin felt no inclination to hit the sack. I thought I'd use the opportunity to find out what they thought of the evening message. The speaker had focused on sin, so I asked, "What do you guys think sin is? How would you define it?"

They tried—they really did. But they were strangers to this theological ground. I was the one who knew that sin could be defined as missing the mark, breaking the law or severing a relationship. They were aware that I was one-up on them. Besides, sin is a rather touchy subject if you feel like anything you say may be used against you. So they "took the Fifth."

Sensing their discomfort, I took a different tack. "What's the average guy at Duarte High School like?" I asked. It took about two minutes of pump-priming to show them that I really wanted to know, but after that it was as if I'd turned on the spigot. They covered how he did in school, how much his father earned, his involvement in sports, the ways he spent his spare time, how much he dated, what he did on a date, whether or not he believed in God or went to church, how he treated others and what he felt guilty about.

The bull session went all over the map with only occasional questions from me. ("Is that right? Do most kids at school get drunk on weekends?") They didn't always agree with each other, but that added to the liveliness. And regardless of what they said, I couldn't contradict them. They knew much more about life as a teen-ager in their town than I did. I'd discovered a topic on which they were the experts.

When we were finished I knew a lot about the typical Duarte student. I also knew a lot about them. As one fellow put it, "Let's face it, Em. We haven't been talking about the average kid. We've been talking about ourselves. When it comes to sin, we're experts!"

I've since learned to phrase questions so as to put the group in a place where they know as much or more about the topic than I. It's not a matter of playing dumb. Rather it's drawing upon their unique experience. For instance, this is a book about leadership. Suppose I wanted to involve a group of readers in a discussion of group leadership. I could ask, "What are the five main principles of discussion leadership?" I could, but getting your thoughts would be like pulling teeth. You'd reason that Em's the one who's written the book. He's supposed to be the pro. Who am I to tell him what will work best? But suppose I set up the discussion this way: "All of us have been involved in a great number of discussions, gabfests, bull sessions. Think back over all the discussions you can recall. Pick the one that was most stimulating, the one where you just had to get in your two-cents worth or you'd burst. It may have been a committee meeting, classroom debate, dorm floor meeting or your family sitting around the dinner table. Try to remember as much about that time as you can. Tell us about that discussion and what you think made it go."

You would be the expert. You were there. I wasn't. Your interpretation of its success is unassailable. I could question and probe, but your view of the experience is the highest court of appeal. We may discover that your conclusions are different from those reached by others. But they were drawing on other situations, so no way could you be wrong! In this supportive climate you'd be motivated to do new thinking about leading a discussion, and in the process I'll be privy to your opinions as you share them with the group. That was the purpose of raising the issue in the first place.

Asking questions so that others are the experts is so crucial to a good discussion that I'll toss out one more example. Suppose you wanted to discuss the attributes of God. You could simply ask the group, "What do you think God is like?" By now you realize the problems with this approach.

On the other hand you could give the issue a different slant—something like this: "Christmas is only a few weeks off. Suppose you came down Christmas morning and discovered a big package under the tree. They say that good things come in small packages, but you've always been partial to the big presents. You eagerly tear off the shiny red paper and discover a genuine do-it-yourself Make-a-God kit. It's not the artificial plastic model, but the authentic original. You read the instructions and discover that you can make any kind of God you want. The only requirement is that once you've made him, you have to live with him. I know this is ridiculous. There is no such thing as a Make-a-God kit. But what if there were? Religious skeptics claim that we make God in our own image. Suppose it were possible to create a god to match our desires. What kind of god would you make?"

I've used this discussion starter a number of times. It's a winner. It's just off-beat enough to stir their curiosity. However people respond, they are correct. They're merely stating their preference, not the state of cosmic truth. In the process I learn a great deal about their views on omnipotence (power), omniscience (knowledge), love, justice and so on. At the same time the group participants start the process of mental churning. I promote this by probing their response. If someone asserts that she'd make God powerful enough to stop all wars, I point out that he'd have enough clout to force his will on them as well. When the discussion centers on God's knowledge, I query them on their willingness to bring into being a god who would know their inner thoughts. The key to this process is crafting questions that make every member an authority. A bit of sanctified imagination will bring it off almost every time.

The Make-a-God-kit example also illustrates a third principle of opening a discussion. *Use vivid imagery.* A few of my colleagues in philosophy claim that we can think in abstractions, but I'm not convinced. If you ask someone to consider the topic of determinism, you're liable to get a blank stare unless he first develops the term into a mental snapshot of a puppeteer pulling strings. People think in pictures. You're ahead if you guide them. Otherwise they may just let abstract terms wash over them without ever engaging in the dialogue.

Make-a-God-kit-type openers help your group think in concrete terms. I've even gone one step further when I've used this one with students. I brought in various shapes of wood—a 2" x 4" labeled Love, a one-inch dowel rod marked Power, a plank with Responsiveness written on it, and so on. When the group agreed on the amount of power they'd give this god, I had them cut the board to a length representing that proportion. Then we nailed the wood together and ended up with a visual representation of their musings.

It's possible to visually portray almost any topic. Our spiritual pilgrimage can be charted over time like the Dow Jones average. Our family relations can be depicted by drawing the seating plan and communication pattern at the dinner table. I've led a Bible study on Mark 4 about Jesus controlling the wind and waves by having participants create a weather map similar to that seen on the evening news. Different areas of the country represent distinct areas of our lives. Traditional symbols for sunny, cloudy, thunderstorms and foggy show how we feel about our work, friends, home life, recreation, God and the like. For any of these issues it's best to start with the nonverbal exercise, and then have people talk about their creation. Most folks are freer to speak up when they can refer to something tangible in their hands.

If you ever want a college group to grapple with the question of how the Lord feels about them, you might suggest they write a letter to themselves from God. Mail is an important event in the lives of college students. It's helpful to get them to picture themselves walking up to their mail box and finding an envelope with no return address. They rip it open and are stunned to find a letter from God. At first they tend to dismiss it as some kind of joke, but the words have the ring of truth. What does it say? I ask

them to follow the format of Jesus' letters to the seven churches
in the book of Revelation.
1. A personalized greeting.
2. God giving himself a special name.
3. Praise for a Christian virtue—some good news.
4. Blame for a specific sin—some bad news.
5. Request for a change.
6. A warning if the request is ignored.
7. A promise if change is made.

Ten minutes of writing can foster a fascinating hour of interchange. Usually there's a building-block effect. As some in the
group see that others are seriously concerned with God's opinion, they in turn get caught up in the quest to discover God's
will. It seems that everyone has trouble verbalizing what God
appreciates about them. Writing a letter from God helps them
picture God saying, "Well done, my good and faithful servant,"
in response to their positive qualities.

In this section on popping the question I've suggested three
guidelines: don't ask value questions with right answers; make
them experts; and set up the issue pictorially. Occasionally you
can create an actual experience for the group that will do all three
in one fell swoop. I wanted our junior-high youth group to consider world hunger and poverty. Coming from affluent homes in
the suburbs they honestly didn't have a frame of reference from
which to start. My wife adapted a program sponsored by World
Vision to fit our situation. We announced that there would be
refreshments during our Wednesday night meeting. We gave
each one a dessert ticket. We had three different kinds and
passed them out at random. In our group of fifty, ten received
a red ticket—good for a piece of fresh strawberry pie. (I sampled
some ahead of time to make sure it was tasty.) When thirty-five
of them turned in their blue tickets they received a graham
cracker. And the five who had brown tickets came up empty.
They got nothing. These proportions roughly parallel the distribution of food in the world. Twenty per cent have great abun-

dance, seventy per cent operate on a subsistence level and ten per cent are starving.

After that brief ten-minute experience we were home free. We couldn't shut them up. Some of those who got the pie shared with their friends. Most didn't. Regardless, each one wanted to explain his or her actions. "If I gave everyone a taste I'd only have a bite myself." The graham cracker contingent was most vocal about the inequities. Those who were shut out were more despairing than angry. "We knew it was hopeless to ask for pie. But it would have been nice to get something." It was easy to bridge from this to questions of world hunger.

Many structured exercises, games and role plays are available commercially.[4] Secular topics include leadership, roles, decision making, crosscultural communication and creativity. Christian-oriented material is available for stimulating discussion about community, spiritual gifts and many of Jesus' encounters with people in the gospels. Both types can be effective because they stay away from simplistic right/wrong answers, provide an experiential base that gives all an equal competence and makes an abstract ideal visual. But you don't need to wait for someone else to create structured experiences for you. You can make up your own discussion starters.

Keeping the Ball Rolling

Starting a discussion is one thing. Keeping it going is another. Your goal is to keep the energy level high. You've taken pains to get the beast off the ground. Now it behooves you to take care not to let the air out of the balloon. Call it what you will—energy, electricity, excitement, dynamism or umph. What follows is a simple list of do's and don'ts that I've found helpful. First the don'ts.

1. Don't judge. You've set up your whole discussion on the premise that there are no right answers. Don't give it the lie by evaluating their comments. I'm at my best when I take a quizzical stance. "You're not wrong, but I'm not sure you're right either."

A gentle probing works wonders—never challenging but in a friendly spirit of curiosity, exploring the depths of what another is saying. If a girl states that she's against war, I try to find out what war. Vietnam? Israel's six-day pre-emptive strike against Egypt? The Allies resistance to Hitler and Tojo in World War 2? It may turn out that there are some conflicts she'll regretfully support.

If a fellow announces categorically that God would never have us lie, I'll mention Rahab the prostitute who lied about the spies she was hiding in the attic. In Hebrews 11 she's praised for her faith. I won't push the point. And there are any number of objections to my example. But chances are my questioning will be an impetus for others to plunge into the discussion.

Put together a group of ten people and on any given issue you'll have ten different opinions, maybe fifteen because sometimes folks are of two minds. I work hard to bring out these variant views without putting anyone on the defensive. As leader, I won't argue. If I can promote a spirited interchange *between* group members, however, I've achieved my aims. A bit of conflict helps people overcome their inhibitions and enter the fray.

2. Don't preach! Many Christian leaders feel an irresistible urge to put in their two cents. Usually it comes across more like a dollar fifty and squelches contributions of others. The best advice I ever received about discussion leading came from a long-time professional in a high-powered business workshop. This one piece of wisdom made the $100 price of admission worthwhile. "Whenever I'm tempted to stick in my own opinion, I shut up. It's the height of arrogance to suppose that others are going to be more interested in hearing my views than they are in expressing their own. So when I feel that gnawing desire to pontificate creeping upon me, I make it a practice to wait at least sixty seconds. By that time I'm usually glad I resisted the impulse to intervene. I suspect the group is even happier."

3. Avoid the detached stance of the scholar. You're the leader. The group will take its cue from you. If you lean back and stroke

your beard (admittedly difficult for some of my readers) as you objectively weigh each thought, the conversation will be dull and halting. If, however, you model excitement, the thing may catch fire.

I try to sit on the edge of a table or desk. I lean forward eagerly when someone speaks. I'm careful not to let my eyes wander. Eye contact says that I'm up for hearing her thoughts. Lack of it would scream out an indifference to the value of her opinion. I'll also nod my head as she continues. If you want to see how effective this is, try an experiment the next time someone shares an idea with you. Nod your head and intersperse your listening with verbal signs of approval: "yes . . . uh-huh . . . that's interesting . . . go on." The words will pour forth in a torrent. Some other time, meet his words with only a blank stare. Or worse yet, solemnly shake your head back and forth and mumble with a sigh, "That's not right." It'll wipe him out. (I suggest you only try this latter experiment with an understanding friend.) Another way to show your interest is to repeat back what was said in your own words. It shows that you were really listening.

All of this takes continual effort. I make sure that I enter a discussion internally fired up, raring to go. For you it may take a cup of coffee, a slap of aftershave or a good night's sleep. Unless the occasion is formal I wear my tennis shoes. Somehow I feel more bouncy. Anything to overcome an impression of indifference. The discussion needs energy. Lethargy is a killer.

4. Plan ahead! It's easy to fall into the trap of not listening to what people are saying because your mind is racing ahead trying to come up with your next question. Preparation is the only way to combat this tendency. It's important that you bone up on a topic so you are ready with illustrations. A discussion of moral choice will go much better if I have a number of Rahab-type ethical dilemmas to trot out at the appropriate time. That kind of mastery takes effort.

An effective discussion takes more preparation time than a speech. In public address I know where I'm going. I start with point A, go to example B and proceed to statement C. It's linear. (See Figure 6A.) I can rehearse the speech until I have it just right. With discussion it's different. There's a geometric progression of options. I start at point A (my opening question) but I don't know for certain whether the group is going to branch off on B, C or D. The possibilities aren't limitless, but good preparation requires that I be ready to react to all contingencies. The actual discussion may go from A to D to M. (See Figure 6B.) But I can't know ahead of time. So I'll have to think through all possible responses ahead of time, even the odd ones. Then I'll be free to

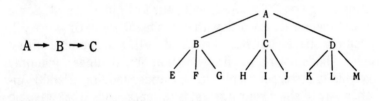

Figure 6A   Figure 6B

concentrate on what the others are saying while avoiding the deadening gaps that often plague a spur-of-the-moment effort.

5. Use humor. I've already stated that conflict enlivens a discussion. It's the same with laughter. Many leaders are afraid to use humor in a religious discussion. That's too bad. I'm firmly convinced that God wants us to take him seriously, but not ourselves. Humor is a great way of releasing tension and keeping things loose. Besides, a discussion should be fun.

I'm not a stand-up comic. I'm a lousy joke teller. But the kinds of humor that help a discussion along are repartee, puns, plays on words, incongruity and exaggeration. Most of us are capable of an occasional comic rejoinder if we have a whimsical attitude ready to spot something ludicrous. If all else fails, poking fun at ourselves guarantees some group mirth.

Don't force it. If you have trouble seeing the funny side of life, you'll appear stilted trying to be something you aren't. But if you have a humorous bent, this is the time to give it full play. One further warning, however. It's easy to slip into a caustic biting humor that tears down group members. Chances are they'll never let you know they're hurt. But the sudden resistance you meet from them and their friends will tell you too late that you've overstepped. When in doubt, err on the side of making yourself the butt of your jokes, not them. It's both effective and Christian.

6. Seek balanced participation. This advice encourages you to deal head on with the two thorniest problems facing a discussion leader: how to get the apathetic person to enter in and how to prevent the monopolizer from dominating the discussion. Both extremes spell trouble.

There's no way you can assess the thoughts of a silent member. But the problem extends beyond that. His silence may have a chilling effect upon others in the group. Suppose you were in a Bible study where people took seriously James's admonition to get into the habit of confessing sins to one another. Nonparticipation of any one member is going to be viewed as a threat to the rest of you. "What's he thinking about me?" you wonder. You'll be less than candid as long as his reactions are a mystery. Also his apparent boredom seems to pass judgment on the worthwhileness of your effort.

But what looks like boredom is often fear. This is especially true in a new group. Remember "flight, fight and unite" from chapter two? During the first phase of a group people are reluctant to get down to business. They are casting about for where they fit, how they can contribute, what they can expect from others. This uncertainty creates tension which contracts facial muscles and tightens vocal chords. So although their minds may be racing with valuable insight, their actual appearance is one stage short of coma.

The standard way of dealing with silent members is to call upon them by name.

"Do you have any ideas, Bill?"

"What's your opinion, John?"

"You haven't said much, Linda."

Unfortunately it usually drives them deeper into their shell. If they are quiet because they are scared of others, singling them out is merely going to increase their fear.

"What do you think, Joan?"

"I think I'd rather be someplace else."

Going around the group so that everyone has a chance to say something doesn't allay the tension. As his or her turn comes closer, the silent member dredges up some innocuous comment. It's the bare minimum designed to shift the group's focus toward someone else. Stimulating discussion it is not.

My approach to dealing with apparent apathy is more indirect. I try to create an atmosphere that is so exciting that people have to share their thoughts or they'll split. All of the things I've talked about earlier in this chapter are designed to contribute to that climate. Controversy, humor, painting word pictures, creating common experiences, a nonjudgmental atmosphere, an informal setting, a high energy level—each of these are goads to overcoming self-consciousness.

I then conduct the discussion in a fashion that could best be described as "planned disorder." I skip such order-producing techniques as hand raising or turn taking, and avoid making comments like, "Shh. Everyone listen to what Sue is saying. If you have something to say share it with the whole group." At times it may seem chaotic. But perhaps the best a silent member can do is to turn to a friend and comment on what someone else said. I don't want to stifle boldness. So I tolerate a wide latitude of whispering, laughing and interruptions in the hopes of activating silent members. In the process I try to be on the alert to the few people who are going to need that extra bit of encouragement to draw them out. Eye contact and an occasional smile are ways of signaling that you're aware of them and that they are special to you.

When you see a flicker of interest or the person makes a side comment to someone else, you can casually extend a hand of invitation and offer, "Do you want in?" This personalized attention is best coupled with an occasional general statement such as, "Remember your idea is as good as the guy next to you— probably better." Or "Let's give some folks who haven't had a chance to say something a shot at the question." There's no guarantee that this indirect strategy will free all members to participate, but at least you know that when people finally speak it's because they want to, not because it was dragged out of them.

Group members who talk too much present a different problem. At first you may be glad for their participation when others are hanging back, but your reaction may soon switch from gratefulness to gritting your teeth. It's not just that their constant chatter is irritating. That you could handle. But when one person takes up fifty per cent of the time, others are getting shut out. They may even decide that crashing in is not worth the effort for fear of appearing as obnoxious Mr. Know-it-all.

Your response to the person who has no unspoken thought will depend on the reason for their talkativeness. It's no use being subtle if they're insensitive to the reactions of the group. Chances are that talking has been their way of getting attention since childhood. (My nickname in junior high was "The Mouth." Not very flattering, but I learned that if I talked long enough and loud enough, people would at least pay attention to me. It was better than being ignored.) The firm approach works best. "Kathy, you've put in some interesting ideas. Now give some other folks a chance."

Sometimes it may be necessary to interrupt a rambling monolog. "Hold it right here, Pete. You're tossing out a number of worthwhile ideas. I'm not sure we can handle all of them at once. Take your first point, boil it down to one simple declarative sentence and we'll see what the others think about it."

Excessive participation may be due to a special interest in the topic. In these cases monopolizing isn't chronic. The person merely gets caught up in a topic that fascinates him or her and

Reprinted with permission from *The* Saturday Evening Post *Company* © 1980

"Protocol or no, if he doesn't stop talking soon, I'm going to eat him."

has a chance to shine. I'll sit on my hands when the subject is Oriental mysticism, but just try to shut me up when we're talking about airplanes, persuasion or a Christian's responsibility to world hunger. A bit of private affirmation will usually bring the amount of participation down to an acceptable level. "Bill, you know a lot more about Sanskrit than others in the group. I'm afraid your knowledge might intimidate them. How about hanging back awhile so others can get in their licks without feeling stupid?" This way you've deputized the monopolizer as an associate discussion leader. Instead of concentrating solely on his own comments, he shares your concern to draw out others.

If there's no chance to talk with him in private, a public comment can accomplish the same effect. "Bill, you've obviously thought a lot about this. Your ideas are pretty well cast into wet cement. That's been helpful for us all. But creativity is a tricky process. Fresh ideas often come from those who are brand new to the problem. Let's see what others have to say." The precise way you do it isn't as important as making sure you intervene. If monopolizers are unchecked, they'll kill the discussion.

Winding It Up

Unfortunately most discussions don't wind up, they wind down. The leader asks plaintively, "Does anybody have anything more to say?" The answer is painfully obvious. This often happens because a discussion goes too long. I'd much rather have an intense fifteen-minute discussion and quit while things are hopping than drag it out to fit a predetermined time frame. My youth pastor helped me see the wisdom in this flexibility. We had a forty-five-minute time slot scheduled for a weekly discussion. He gave me a wide latitude. I especially appreciated his permission to fail. "Kids are unpredictable. Sometimes they'll come on like gangbusters. Other times they'll sit and vegetate. If it's not going, cut it off. No use making everyone miserable. If things catch fire, go on longer. My experience is that only one out of three discussions goes. So don't worry if you have a few losers."

I'm often asked about the best way to summarize a discussion at the end. My advice is simple. Don't.[5]

A summary has about three things going against it. The main drawback is that it has a calming effect. It ties everything into a package. This imagery is reflected in typical discussion terminology. The summary is the time for "wrapping up." There are no loose ends. Folks can relax now because the topic which seemed so uncertain and turbulent is now reduced to a neat list of principles that won't bother anyone. They can go home now with an unfurrowed brow.

But you don't want that! The whole purpose of the discussion was to stimulate. You'd much rather see folks walk out of the room arguing, churning with things yet to say, bothered by ideas they heard. The best way to accomplish this is to simply end while things are going well. "Hey, that's it. This has really been good. See you next week." Better to leave a few folks agitated by quitting too soon than to miss a good stopping point.

Another problem with a summary is that it never catches the full flavor of what's been said. How could it? When you try to capture all the diverse elements of an hour-long discussion in a three-minute synthesis, something is bound to be lost. Ideas get truncated, sharp edges blurred. I may have spoken only twice, but I remember best what I said. If my ideas are missing in the summary, I feel gypped. Even if I spot them, I feel ticked that you didn't understand their full nuance. It's a no-win situation.

Finally, there's the ever-present problem of evaluation lurking just below the surface. Although it's theoretically possible to summarize in a purely descriptive fashion, judgment almost always creeps in. People have long memories. You've stated up front that there are no right answers. If your mood and manner at the end give those words the lie, it can be fatal the next time you try to get folks to open up. They figure you'll give the "true word" at the end, and so sit back aloof and wait for you to lay it on them. Of course none of these thoughts about summaries apply if you've had a problem-solving session and need to conclude by crystallizing the decisions the group has made. But that sort of discussion was dealt with in chapter four on decision making.

A Group Must Have Its Say

Like any field, group leadership is laced with pompous-sounding jargon. My favorite is "quality dialogical interface." It merely means a good talk between two people. As stilted as the phrase sounds, it would be a shame to let it mask the truth to which it refers. To be a whole we must have someone listen to us. Who we are, where we've been, what we think, how we feel are vitally important. If no one will listen, we are nothing. No matter how talented and powerful a leader you are, you won't be effective unless you find ways to let your group have its say. One-way communication has gone the way of the dodo bird—at least it should.

Leading a discussion is tough. It would be easy to try out some of the ideas in this chapter once, fall flat on your face and then revert back to the safety of straight lecture. But that's not an option for sensitive leaders. They know that the only way they'll find out what folks are thinking is to ask them. Sometimes it's risky finding out. It's even more risky not to know.

Part Three
Relationships
in
Groups

6

Self-Disclosure

In my first year of high school I double-dated with my older sister and her boyfriend. We were at a coffee shop when Ralph commented that I looked flushed. As a matter of fact I did feel hot and headachy as well. He also pointed out that my face had broken out during the night even more than my case of teen-age acne would warrant. When I admitted that the lights in the restaurant seemed a bit bright he announced the obvious—I had measles.

This was a blow. Our family was scheduled to go on a Florida vacation the next morning. We knew that as soon as our parents discovered my illness they would cancel the trip. So we conspired not to let them know. I took aspirin for the headache, covered my arms with long-sleeve shirts, and wore dark glasses outside. I stayed out of the sun and used generous quantities of talcum powder and Clearasil to mask the worst blemishes on my face. My folks never found out.

This extreme example represents my basic philosophy toward self-disclosure as I grew up. It was summed up in the motto: "Don't tell Mom!" Early patterns die hard. Whenever I experience strong emotions my initial impulse is to put a close guard on my words and label my feelings TOP SECRET.

I now feel another pull, however. I am a college professor, youth leader in my church, Young Life national board member and father. I know the loneliness of leadership in each of these roles. I find myself uncomfortable adopting a detached stance. I have a strong desire to take others into my confidence—openly reporting what's going on inside me. Transparency seems to offer a warm option to my aloof attitude. But will this be best for me and the people I serve?

I'm torn, and I find that I'm not alone. The world can be a scary place. We're hesitant to share our innermost thoughts with others. Some are willing to commit their hopes and frustrations to the pages of a diary. But the diary has a lock and is stored in a private place. Even prayer doesn't fulfill our desperate need to be known and loved by other warm human beings. But still we hold back. Why? John Powell answers that question simply in his book, *Why Am I Afraid To Tell You Who I Am?* "Because if I tell you who I am, you may not like who I am, and it's all that I have."[1]

Being a Christian does not automatically make it easier to reveal our true selves. Because we have some God-given standards of what life should be, it may be even harder to let others glimpse the person inside. I had a professor in seminary who claimed that there's more fellowship in the average bar than there is in the Christian church. He went on to suggest that we take seriously the advice of James. "You should get into the habit of admitting your sins to each other" (Jas 5:16 Phillips).

This was my first touch with someone who recommended a systematic program of self-disclosure. I was intrigued by the idea. I shared my excitement with a fellow student in the lunch line after class. "Aw, that's nothing new," he said. "My roommate and I have a pact. I tell him his sins and he tells me mine." This kind of judgment makes most Christians leery of self-disclosure. We're afraid of getting dumped on. And we have a sneaking suspicion that God's opinion is reflected in human judgment. Christian leaders have an additional worry. Won't it invalidate our ministry if our followers know what we are really like? It seems safest to merely pray and keep our own counsel. So we normally give away very little.

This raises a question. Is the normal person necessarily a healthy person? A number of psychologists would say no. Sidney Jourard believes that most people have a tough time sharing the deep parts of their lives with even one other person. The body pays the price of silence. Headaches, back pains, ulcers, colitis, high blood pressure are forms of protest. They are tilt signals—indications that something is out of kilter. Jourard sees these and other illnesses stemming from the lack of self-disclosure.

In thinking about health, I like to conjure up the image of a family of germs looking for a home in which they might multiply and flourish. If I were the leader of such a family of germs and had the well-being of my family at heart, I would avoid any man like the plague so long as he was productively and enjoyably engaged in living and loving. I would wait until he lost hope, or became discouraged, or became ground down by the requirements of respectable role-playing. At that precise moment, I would invade; his body would then become as fertile a life-space for my breed of germs as a well-manured flowerbed is for the geranium or the weed.[2]

Jourard advocates taking the risk of sharing our attitudes, reactions, loves, fears and background with at least one significant other person. He believes that a more transparent life will promote intrapersonal and interpersonal well-being. Do I agree? That's what the rest of this chapter is about. At this point I can only give a tentative yes. I'll first present the benefits of self-disclosure as I see them, and then sketch the possible drawbacks. I'll conclude by suggesting some things that can be done to avoid the pitfalls of inappropriate disclosure.

Benefits

Self-disclosure usually draws us closer to those who listen. To my mind this is the greatest effect of transparency. There's no guarantee that it will work that way every time. People can get turned off when they hear too much, too fast, from too many. But there's no question that a certain amount of openness is a necessary precondition for interpersonal intimacy. Breadth and depth of self-revelation is still the most reliable indication of the level of friendship. This relational fact of life has some tragic implications for those who have unfulfilled needs for affiliation. Loners are hesitant to take off their masks for fear of rejection. This very act of concealment, however, is destined to block the closeness they desperately desire. It's a vicious circle that recalls Christ's words, "For to him who has will more be given; and from him who has not, even what he has will be taken away" (Mk 4:25).

It's not clear why personal sharing fosters attraction. It may be that people discover just how similar they are—brothers under the skin. Research has demonstrated that we like those who are like us.[4] Or perhaps it's a response to the gift of trust that's inherent in self-revelation. I feel privileged when you let me in on something close to you. It makes for a special bond. Both of these explanations are important to people in leadership positions. Pastors, teachers, executives and even parents tend to be separated from their people by a status gap. Appropriate self-disclosure is a way of bridging that gulf. Leaders set the tone for the level of openness in their group. If they are private people, reserved, members will hold back. But if they model an unguarded transparency, people will be freed to pursue intimacy. That's why this chapter on self-disclosure is part of the relationship section.

One of my favorite movies of the last decade was *The Sting*. Robert Redford and Paul Newman play two Depression-era con men who bilk a big-time New York mobster out of a million dollars. They go to fantastic lengths to carry out their deception. The continuous tension makes the film entertaining for the spectator through the final reel. One little slip at an unguarded moment will bring the whole ruse crashing down on them. What strikes me most is the fantastic psychic energy required to live a lie. Honest self-disclosure can relieve this tension. I can relax if I don't need to constantly monitor what parts of my life I metered out to which people.

Pastors and counselors have known for years that tension release accompanies self-disclosure. Clients come to them for "the talking cure." They seek a sympathetic ear, not advice. By honestly revealing their inner life they leave feeling more whole. This is unique in the health profession. I know of no claim that taking blood pressure will cure people of hypertension. Yet taking the pulse of the soul not only monitors mental health, the very act often brings relief. This same release is equally available when talking to a friend over coffee as it is in a professional's office at $50/hour.

There's a third benefit. We become known. A high-school girl brought this home to me. After leading a Young Life club for a decade I announced one night that I was in my final year Laura came up after the meeting in tears. She said, "Oh, Em, I m so sad. Now we won't get to know each other." I tried to soothe her by pointing out that we went to the same church and that I was friends with her folks. I assured her that she'd have ample opportunity in the future to get to know me. "That's not it," she responded. "I want you to get to know me."

Christians have a special need to be known. It's natural for those of us with moral sensitivity to conclude that we invented sin. When those guilt feelings hit I have a hard time believing God forgives unless I first experience that forgiveness from some warm bodies here on earth. But even that acceptance is hollow unless I've been transparent enough to know that people see the real me—warts and all. Otherwise I'll figure they only can love me because they don't really know how rotten I am. Being open and honest with others gives me the assurance that no matter how people react to me, they're responding to the genuine article, not some spruced-up version.

Self-disclosure offers a fourth plus. In the process of letting someone else get to know me, I discover who I am. You'd think it would work the other way around—that I'd first figure out who I am, and then let others in on the secret. But they're often simultaneous. Paul Tournier, the noted Swiss physician, states that we can't get to know ourselves through introspection.[5] Introspection is like peeling the skin off of an onion. You remove layer after layer and discover there's nothing left.

Tournier claims that dialogue with others is the only true route to self-knowledge. Self-awareness is a by-product of the struggle to honestly expose my being to someone else. He practices what he preaches. Recently this famous Christian doctor and writer invited a group of Wheaton College students to have tea. They were overwhelmed at the personal time and effort he invested in the preparation and serving of the food. Couldn't these hours have been spent more profitably in writing or something more important than talking with some college kids he'd never known before and might never see again? Not according to Tournier. He simply said, "There is nothing more important than honest dialogue between Christians. It's how we discover ourselves, our friends and our God."

I've listed a number of reasons for revealing ourselves to others. These are compelling ideas to me. But there's obviously another side to the story. Otherwise we would live in a totally transparent world, and there would be no call for a chapter on self-disclosure. Prudence requires that we examine the possible pitfalls involved in openness.

Drawbacks
Self-disclosure can boomerang. Folks may get a glimpse of what I'm really like and decide they want no part of me. My little foibles or peculiarities may prove endearing, but friends could be driven away if they spot the garbage in my life. Research findings con-

firm that overdisclosure can dampen attraction.[6] We don't need a laboratory study to convince us. We avoid the bore who wants to discuss every detail of his latest operation. And perhaps that's our gnawing fear—that others won't find our self-disclosure shocking, merely tedious.

Negative reactions would hurt. Yet more distressing is the possibility that what we've told in private may be leaked in public. Our words could come back to clobber us later. When I was in seventh grade I told a new friend about one of my hobbies— building miniature ballparks. I'd lay out the foul lines with chalk on the carpet, erect the outfield fences with building blocks, and fashion the double-deck stands with materials from a steel-girder construction set. I was able to copy the dimensions of Wrigley Field and build a replica of Comiskey Park—complete with working light towers. I felt a slight embarrassment over this pursuit. Somehow it didn't seem quite manly. The day after I told Don it was all over school. Em was doing something weird with Tinker Toys.

The professional recipients of secrets in our society are doctors, lawyers and priests. They are sworn to uphold an ethic of confidentiality. Only rarely is this obligation violated. But there's a greater chance of exposure when we entrust our confidences to a casual friend. To some the cash value of a secret comes when it is spilled to others.

Another danger of self-disclosure is that people have been hurt by our candor. The term *brutal honesty* has come to describe the bludgeoning technique of telling others things for their own good. When the offended party objects, the insensitive talker responds self-righteously, "I was only being honest." I've experienced this kind of openness before and didn't like it, and don't want to offend others this way. I knew one woman who censored nothing. If I walked into the room and she didn't like my tie, she'd say so for all to hear. To be fair, she was just as quick to announce her approval. People she knew tended to forgive her bluntness as eccentric behavior. But if hurting people is central to self-disclosure, I want no part of it.

Others balk at the idea of voluntarily giving away what they consider their greatest personal resource—privacy. These include South American Indians that object to being photographed, believing that the camera has robbed them of a portion of their essence. Greta Garbo voiced the desire of many: "I want to be alone." Seclusion became an obsession to Howard Hughes, though not many go to such extremes. But a significant number of people regard solitude as healthy. They figure there's a good chance they'll regret tomorrow the words carelessly bestowed today. Along this line, some leadership theorists maintain that there's an optimum distance between leader and follower. If leaders become too familiar, they'll lose some of the mystique that makes them effective.

There's an attack on the whole concept of self-disclosure that is quite different than those discussed above. It comes from some Evangelicals who are suspicious of the philosophical roots of humanistic psychology. They look at some of the leading proponents of openness and honesty in human relations—Carl Rogers, Erich Fromm, Rollo May, Abraham Maslow. They see these men advocating:

Unconditional acceptance—which seems to be ethically bankrupt.

Self-love—which they label narcissistic and/or idolatrous.

The basic goodness of man—which plays fast and loose with the concept of sin. Other Christians don't want to toss out the idea of transparency, but they're disturbed by the cult of confessionalism which has a great willingness to report sin, but makes little effort to repent from it.

Self-disclosure is neither an unmitigated blessing nor an automatic curse. All things being equal, I'll opt for transparency. But the question of whether to reveal personal history, private thoughts and hidden emotions is not one of either/or. Rather it's one of appropriateness.

Appropriateness can be viewed from three different angles. One perspective has to do with the recipient of your openness— the *who*. It makes sense to differentiate between those who will lend a sympathetic ear and those who can't handle intimate discussion. The timing of self-disclosure is a second consideration —the *when*. The right time and place will make both parties feel more comfortable. Finally there's the matter of how much honesty—the *what*. Some things may be best unsaid. Others need airing. In the rest of this chapter I want to explore the who, when and what aspects of appropriate self-disclosure. In other words, how can we maximize the benefits of openness while minimizing the drawbacks?

Who

We're easily fed up with the game playing, hiding behind masks and phoniness in the world. It's tempting to throw up our hands in despair and commit ourselves to spill our guts to everyone. But we can't. It's impossible to establish a meaningful relationship with a tollbooth collector. The results would be a monumental traffic jam. Most of our relationships are destined to be governed by roles—the social lubricant which makes normal interaction possible. We can and should play things straight with all people, but intimate self-disclosure needs be reserved for the few. We have only so much time and psychic energy. By the very nature of this limitation we have to pick and choose. Extended sharing with one person precludes in-depth openness with another.

Who should we choose? *Someone we trust.* It would be folly for a player in a high-stakes poker game to show his hand since the other players are each out to do him in. Likewise, we'd be wise not to bare our soul to competitive group members who see our loss as their gain. By contrast there are people who have our best interest at heart. As part of a Christian community they feel forgiven and are comfortable with themselves. Slow to judge, members of the group unconditionally accept us for who we are, even if they don't agree with all of our actions. They aren't eager to persuade us to change. Anytime you run across a group radiating this kind of warmth, it's worth taking the risk of self-disclosure.

Confidentiality is part of trust. True confidants are those who know how to keep their mouths shut. You'd think that getting burned on the disclosing end would make us doubly careful not to violate the trust implicit in a shared secret. But reality compels us to recognize that we often get sloppy in holding a confidence. It's not always easy to spot those who can keep their own counsel from those who will give in to the temptation to gossip. Discretion is a cultivated response—it's not innate.

Returning to the poker analogy—prudence dictates that we not bet more than we can afford to lose. This means placing a tentative trust in people and checking on how they handle it. If trust is violated, we will be sadder but wiser. If they respect our privacy, we can then entrust them with more of who we are. It's reminiscent of Christ's statement, "You have been faithful over a little, I will set you over much" (Mt 25:21, 23).

A well-known fact of sharing is called the bus-rider phenomenon. People often prefer to bare their soul to a stranger rather than to a lifelong friend. The reason is obvious. I'll probably never see my Greyhound seatmate again, so there's no risk in sharing my innermost hopes and fears. Although this kind of self-disclosure affords a degree of catharsis—getting things off our chest—it doesn't give us any of the interpersonal benefits listed earlier. Besides, it's risky. How do we know that person isn't a friend of a friend? Often the temporary relief of "letting it all hang out" to a stranger is overshadowed by doubts and embarrassment the morning after. It's much more satisfying to select a listener with whom we have an ongoing relationship.

Reprinted by permission © 1981 NEA, Inc.

"Excuse me! Mind if I sit next to you and tell you my whole life story?"

I'm fortunate to have my pastor as my best friend. We've been close for ten years. Every week we'll spend an hour and a half in the steam room at the local YMCA. The continuing nature of our friendship means that the intimate details of my life that swirl together with the vapor are heard in the context of mutual responsibility to each other. He's lucky too. Although I'm active in the youth program of our church, I don't serve as an elder or deacon. My only assignment is this unofficial "steam room committee." He can use me as a confessor, cheerleader or sounding board for ideas. Because we have a history of many soggy hours together, neither of us feels "on stage" with each other.

My wife and I have experienced this same accountability with other couples at a marriage retreat. Six couples shared struggles of faith, vocation, sex, money, conflict and parenting between themselves and among each other. Self-disclosure wasn't cheap. Material shared would still be known by those important to us a week later. It placed an emphasis on authenticity.

This example raises the question of group encounter. A number of organizations like Faith at Work, Fellowship House and Serendipity have risen up to promote authentic self-disclosure among Christians. Is it appropriate to open up in a group of people as opposed to a private one-on-one relationship? The answer may be a matter of personal taste. I have received a great deal of insight and affirmation from koinonia-type groups. One caution is in order, though. Group sharing is healthy only when participation is voluntary. It's possible to use social pressure to force a person to open up. This demand is often prefaced with the claim, "The group has a right to know." But groups don't have rights— only individuals do. We must protect a person's right to remain silent even if it makes us feel uncomfortable. Anyone familiar with the encounter-group movement has heard war stories about emotional breakdowns being triggered by group experience. Enforced sharing is not only unethical, it's the main cause of group casualties.

Appropriateness dictates that we have a sliding scale of disclosure. Jesus revealed much about himself to the multitudes, but a great deal went unsaid or was masked in parables. The disciples heard more. But only the inner circle of Peter, James and John got to view Jesus on the Mount of Transfiguration. We need to differentiate among those who hear our disclosure, and we also must be sensitive to the times when they can't handle our truth. "I have yet many things to say to you, but you cannot bear them now" (Jn 16:12). This is not the despairing cry of a rejected leader but the discerning observation of one who is attuned to others.

When

I have a poster on my office wall that pictures a stylishly drawn turtle with an elongated neck. The caption reads: "Behold the turtle who makes progress only when he sticks his neck out." Many advocates of self-disclosure use the turtle as an example of what *not* to be—retreating into your shell because you're afraid to expose yourself to others. But I see this funny-looking creature as a model of what appropriate disclosure should be. I picture two turtles, face to face, except their heads are almost completely hidden from view. One turtle extends his neck just a bit. It'd be foolish to stick it out all the way—he might get his head lopped off. If the other turtle responds in kind then the first one ventures out some more. In a series of minute movements the turtle ends up with his head in the sunshine, but only if his counterpart follows his lead. At any time he's prepared to slow the progression, come to a complete stop or even back off.

There are a number of salient features in my turtle picture. First and foremost is reciprocity. At best self-disclosure is not a solo act. There is a quid pro quo. "You tell me your dream; I'll tell you mine." The healthiest form of self-presentation is probably that which is just slightly ahead of the norm. Figure 7 pictures the relationship.

I've tried to capture this idea in the image of my turtle. He takes the initial risk. He's always a tad ahead of the game—test-

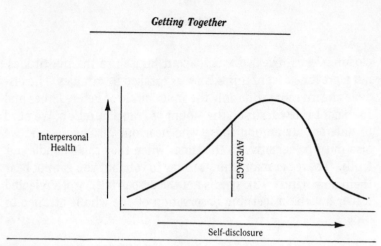

Figure 7

ing, probing, hoping. That kind of risk is tied into self-esteem. A person with a low self-image will be scared of the potential scorn from others, and therefore remain silent. But people who have a modicum of self-confidence won't feel like their whole existence hangs in the balance, so they can afford to chance it. But at the same time they are constantly monitoring others' responses and are ready to pull back when confronted with indifference or hostility.

Reciprocity is crucial as an indication of the other's internal state of mind. It signals that he's not offended by our initial revelation. Even more important, it shows a willingness to be vulnerable. There's a parity of risk. I've got the goods on him just as much as he does on me. There's a good probability he'll be trustworthy. Finally it reveals a readiness to proceed to deeper levels of intimacy.

The turtle model also focuses on the gradual nature of appropriate self-disclosure. It takes time. Fortunately, proponents of "instant intimacy" are on the decline. I'm not a wine drinker, but the idea of an old vintage patiently aged in wooden casks holds a certain appeal. Stress conditions can accelerate the friendship process, but the normal pattern is one of slow growth.

The tortoise imagery doesn't speak to the question of public

"Aw, come on out. Everybody's been asking for you."

self-disclosure. Is there a warrant for a leader to spread his or her life out like an open book in the pulpit, classroom or office? If my own experience is any indication, yes. In 1976 I published *The Mind Changers.* I included many personal examples to illustrate my points. I've received a number of letters from people who've read the book. The theme of the correspondence is invariably the same: "Thanks for being willing to reveal who you are."

Groups often place their leaders on a pedestal. Self-disclosure helps them come down from that uncomfortable position and become warm human beings who laugh, sweat, are afraid and go to the bathroom just like everybody else. It's a trade-off. What they lose in status, they gain in approachability. Of course some leaders can't afford to give up any perceived competence. They're already regarded by their people as bumblers. Many Americans saw Jerry Ford as a nice guy who was over his head in the Presidency. Every time he would stumble or bump his head coming out of a plane people would recall Lyndon Johnson's biting jest that Ford couldn't walk and chew gum at the

127

same time. When a leader's authority is in question, self-revelation could be counterproductive. But when his competence is recognized, vulnerability is a strength.

What

The leading survey of self-disclosure habits breaks down the concept into six subcategories:[7]

Attitudes—toward religion, sex, drinking, communism, beauty in women, etc.

Tastes—favorite movies, books, food, spare-time activities, etc.

Work—dreams and ambitions, what task most favored, weaknesses, strains, etc.

Money—net worth, salary, amounts owed, budget, etc.

Personality—self-concept, guilts, worries, etc.

Body—idealized vision, what ashamed of, health, etc.

We can use this as a check list to investigate the idea of breadth and depth.

Depth refers to the amount of risk involved in sharing. It's easier to tell you about what I like most in my work than about my job weaknesses. To most people it's harder to present negative data than it is to share their victories and virtues. But risk goes beyond embarrassment. It also refers to openness to change. There's little risk involved in proclaiming, "I love sugar! I always have and I always will. There's no use trying to get me to change —that's just the way I am." That kind of presentation leaves little room for argument. Consider, however, the heightened cost of stating it like this: "I'm afraid I'm hooked on sugar. I can't get enough of the stuff. Perhaps I should try to cut down on my sugar intake. What are your thoughts?" Here the speaker is tentative and indicates a willingness to change. Groups can facilitate this willingness by refusing to be shocked by what others share. Acceptance begets more self-disclosure and a greater openness to change.

Breadth has to do with the range of topics discussed. It's possible to go very deep in one area but barely touch the surface in another. I might tell you all about my passion for flying (taste), but avoid mentioning that I fear I might not pass my next flight physical (body). Summer romances are famous for intensity, but often both parties neglect to clue in each other on the basic demographic details of who they are. Many Christians are eager to share their religious beliefs but draw a line around financial matters. It seems to me that self-disclosure is most appropriate when its range and level of intimacy go together. Breadth without depth is superficiality. But depth without breadth gives only the illusion of self-disclosure without the reality.

The disclosure index presented above doesn't tap into personal history. It concentrates on the here and now as opposed to the there and then. But since our roots give insight into who we are, those desiring to be transparent will want to reveal some of their background.

After dinner each night at the two-week island seminar on group dynamics, one of the eight participants takes thirty minutes to an hour to present the significant past events that have shaped him or her into the person they are now. We call it, "This Is Me." There's no question that this exercise does more to leap-frog the group into an intimate knowledge of one another than any other activity we do. The success of this sharing is partially due to the fact that I go first. I try to model a comfortable depth of sharing that will free others from their inhibitions. Disclosure begets disclosure.

Another reason for its effectiveness is the distinction we've discovered between *history* and *story*. History is a bare-bones recitation of facts about my past. If I tell you, for instance, that my older brother died of pneumonia before I was born, that's history. It's quite possible you will shrug your shoulders and voice a mental, "So what?" But if I tell you that my parents were deathly afraid that I'd catch cold and dressed me in a snowsuit when it was 45°, that's the beginning of story. It's even more helpful when I tie this in with my present casual disregard for preventative health measures. I've interpreted the facts and told how they've affected me. Story is a big hunk of what self-disclosure is all about.

No discussion of content would be complete without a focus on emotions. Feelings are the great leveler of human existence. You may have been raised on a farm, earned a Ph.D. in theology, vote Republican and enjoy golf. I may be a product of the inner city, a devout atheist, drive a fork lift at a box factory, agitate for social reform and be a bowling nut. We disagree in starting point, method and conclusion. Yet we both taste the fear of rejection, the surge of sexual attraction, the weariness of responsibility and the warmth that comes with affirmation. Since all are equal on the gut level, feelings are the common currency of self-disclosure.

Emotions are like the ocean surf—powerful, exciting and often scary. There's a natural tendency to self-inject a mental Novocain that will numb our passion and dampen our fear. That's too bad. I agree with John Powell's approach to handling emotion: "Emotions are not moral, neither good nor bad in themselves. If I am to tell you who I really am I must tell you about my feelings whether I will act upon them or not. With rare exceptions emotions must be reported at the time they are being experienced."[8]

This is easy to say but hard to do. I was in a sharing group with students in my school when I felt a stab of bitter jealousy toward another professor. Consistent with what Powell says, I don't see the initial impulse of envy as sin. But I was long past that stage. I had held in this jealousy quite awhile, letting it fester into a grudge and even nurturing it. That's sin. I was caught in a dilemma. Green-eyed envy isn't a socially acceptable reaction in my fellowship. My discomfort was compounded by the fact that the teacher's wife was a member of the group. Dare I admit my jealousy in front of her? Maybe I should just keep quiet —or at least wait till she was gone.

I don't know what tipped the balance, but somewhat haltingly

I reported my feeling. The reaction was immediate. She laughed, but not in derision. It turned out that her husband that very morning had confessed to her that he coveted my ease with students. My jealousy vanished immediately. Wouldn't it have been sad if I'd held it in and nurtured a grudge? It would be even more tragic—and sinful—if I'd given into resentment and cut him down in front of students. Prompt reporting of the emotion was the better part of wisdom. My goal is to act as wisely in the future.

The jealousy I just spoke of was *my* problem, not his. But what if someone does things that are irksome? Perhaps he talks with his mouth full or boasts so much about his accomplishments that others are turned off. Does honest self-disclosure involve sharing our irritation? The answer, I think, depends on the nature of our relationship. My standard is this: I stick to compliments unless the other person has in some way asked for negative feedback. I have no call to pop somebody's balloon unless he or she indicated a willingness to hear my criticism.

There are a variety of ways people might signal that they are up for negative feedback. Close friendship is one. The other day I told my steam-room friend that his breath smelled of garlic. He thanked me, and I think he really meant it. The trust we've built up in the past took the sting out of my words. A direct request can also give permission for an accurate appraisal. I read the first draft of this chapter to my class and asked for comments. I stressed my desire for criticism so that I could make it better. After an awkward pause one fellow said, "Well, as long as you asked, . . ." and initiated a string of helpful suggestions. An honest work relationship is often the arena for constructive criticism. Our commitment to quality work is an implicit warrant for accuracy over flattery. Of course there may come a time when my actions go beyond the point of being merely bothersome. If through ignorance or malice I start to hurt people, simple human justice requires that you speak out.

In all of the cases above it's important to state our opinion as just that—our opinion as opposed to truth thundered down from Mt. Olympus. "You're a prude!" is not nearly as helpful as, "I get the impression that you're embarrassed when we speak of sex." Since honesty is just one arrow in our interpersonal arsenal, a certain tentativeness is appropriate. Sharing our perceptions is more loving than announcing our judgments. God's first call is not to worship honesty but to love.

Occasionally love will leave a few things unsaid. Some are matters of simple kindness. Suppose a friend displays her newborn baby and proudly asks, "How do you think he looks?" You are reminded of a wrinkled prune, but it would be cruel to say so. Other occasions pose heavy moral dilemmas. A friend has committed adultery. He experienced a tremendous load of guilt, and after months of agonizing confessed to his wife. He felt better, but she was devastated. The knowledge of his unfaithfulness and the rejection it implied wracked her for years. From my standpoint he would have done better to keep silent. His sin was infidelity, not in keeping it secret. Forgiveness came through repentance. Broadcasting the act only compounded the harm.

I hate to close on this note, however, for I'm convinced that most of us err on the side of nondisclosure. We constrict our circle of confidants, fail to recognize situations where openness is appropriate and censor thoughts that would be quite acceptable. It's natural to be cautious. But we of all people have reason to open more of our lives to public view. Jesus is our model. "Do not merely look out for your own personal interests, but also for the interests of others. Have this attitude in yourselves which was also in Christ Jesus, who, although He existed in the form of God, did not regard equality with God a thing to be grasped, but emptied Himself . . ." (Phil 2:4-7 NASB).

Self-disclosure is a form of kenosis—self-emptying. Yet it's possible to reveal who we are in a way that includes others rather than voiding our person. I've listed self-disclosure guidelines of what, when and to whom that will help insure that no one in the group gets burned.

There's one very positive aspect of our native reticence to be open. It reminds us that others are just as scared of honesty as we are. Because it's tough for us, we can appreciate the raw courage that lies behind another's struggle to be transparent. This risk and the need to respond tenderly is captured in Louise White's words:

The cards are down—
seven secret stacks.

This game was started long ago
before I knew you.

The gamble is a big one;
All that I am
For all that I can be.

I know the cards on top;
Those I can see and handle quickly.
But as long as cards underneath
lie unturned, unknown,
I cannot win.

Do I play against myself
or
with myself?

Do not tell me, please,
to play the red eight on the black nine.

Just sit with me as I hesitate,
And wait as I wait.
I cannot hurry,
For I have so much more at stake than you.[9]

From The Experience of Psychotherapy *by W. H. Fitts.* ©*1965 by D. Van Nostrand. Reprinted by permission.*

7
Conflict

Our Inter-Varsity chapter in college loved to sing. I think our favorite song was "Praise the Savior." But I never cared for one of the stanzas.

Jesus is the name that charms us
He for conflict fits and arms us . . .

I don't like conflict. I'm not alone in that aversion. Most of us would just as soon avoid hassle. This is especially true for Christian leaders. Friction between people seems to sap much of our energy. We sigh and dream about an idyllic world where there are no disputes. But conflict is a fact of life. It's not a matter of deciding whether or not you will allow its presence in your group. It's already there. The question is how you're going to deal with it. I'm not even sure that a society void of conflict is the best of all possible worlds. Some good things happen because it's there.

First, it keeps things from getting boring. Maybe dullness isn't a problem for your group, but it is in many. There's nothing like a good argument to stir up the juices and keep things hopping. Then again it can stimulate needed change. A classic report on protest in the United States since the Revolution concludes that no social advance has taken place without heated dispute.[1] As believers we have a desire to know Truth. It is only when thoughts see the light of day in the free marketplace of ideas that they can be examined for their biblical soundness. This means conflict, for you may have noticed that not all Christians agree. It's also important that we exercise our spiritual muscles. If we never have any practice in dealing with discord, we may be bowled over when confronted by major disagreement. By working with it in small doses we won't be so uncomfortable when the big blow hits.

Finally, there are personal benefits to open conflict in groups. There's no question that down deep we occasionally get mad. If we never let any of that anger out, we're like a walking time bomb. Someone's liable to get hurt. Dealing openly with conflict is therapeutic. Once the anger is out front there's the joy that can come from reconciliation. Making up is half the fun. So conflict can either be the capstone or the curse of group life. When dealt with constructively, it will draw people together into a cohesive whole as nothing else can do. But if conflict is botched or ignored it can drive a permanent wedge between members. Relationships in groups rise and fall on the basis of how people handle conflict.

Old patterns die hard. I probably haven't convinced you that conflict is the greatest thing since the invention of the tubeless tire. But like death and taxes it will always be with us, so let's take a look at what causes it and then consider different strategies for handling rifts. To illustrate I've picked an ongoing dispute for this bearded college prof. Giving and grading tests.

I like to think of myself as a reasonably competent teacher. I trust this isn't mere self-delusion. Student critiques, peer evaluations and comments from my superiors are all complimentary. But somehow I've built a reputation for giving impossible exams. This isn't an honor I covet. I wouldn't mind it if I was thought of as "hard but fair." But many students regard my testing method as "nit-picky," "frustrating" and even "destructive." No question about it—we've got a conflict. Let's see how it got that way.

Status Gap

It's possible that most of the anger my students feel is due to the age-old battle with authority. Father-son, boss-worker, teacher-student—the arena may differ but the struggle is the same. No one likes to be under the thumb of someone else. My students feel helpless. I make the assignments, decide when and how they'll be tested and then deal out grades with apparent whim. They want in on the process, to have a say on how their fate is decided. Yet the deck of power is stacked in my favor. This is especially galling when they're at the time of life of breaking from the authority of their parents. From this point of view, a bit of rebellion is natural. If they never moaned and groaned, you'd worry about their sanity.

Once a fellow told me he wanted to take the course pass/fail. I had previously announced that I didn't like students doing that because they sloughed off in their work. Since the course had a long waiting list, I wanted people who were ready to dig in. Steve insisted that he had a right to sign up for the nongraded option. I conceded that right, but told him that since he had an overall A- average, he'd have to do B work for me to certify that he'd passed. Anything less would be a mockery. He complained to the academic dean who called me and gave me the word: "According to the student handbook, Steve's right. If he does work that would normally earn a D, you have to pass him. Sorry about that, Em. I can see your point of view. But that's the way it is." You can imagine my reaction. Steve had brought in the big guns and shot me down. Power struggles cause conflict.

There's a problem with status difference as the sole explana-

"We younger fleas demand a bigger say in the running of this dog."

tion of our differences, however. First, not all profs on campus stir up the same amount of test anguish. Some teachers I respect greatly have established cordial grading procedures. It also makes it too easy to duck responsibility for the irritation. I can just shrug off any criticism with a snide, "You-know-what-students-are-like" type of comment. I'll never come to grips with the fact that the real problem may lie with me. It could be that I write lousy tests or have unreasonable expectations. Despite these qualifications there's no doubt that a status difference tends to drive a wedge between folks.

Torn between Two Roles

Wouldn't life be simple if we only had one thing to do? Boring, but simple. Such is not the case. As a teacher I have many functions. One that I regard as crucial is "Friend of the Student." It's not enough for me to be current in my subject or an interesting lecturer. This means disclosing who I am. It means caring about their career plans, social life and emotional well-being. I find that the closer I get to a student, the harder it is to give him or her a poor grade. I try to keep my integrity in this matter. I announce at the start of the term that I can assign a poor grade and still think well of a person. But there's no question that personal involvement exerts pressure.

I have another role. The college expects me to be "Protector of Academic Standards." Throughout academia grade inflation is on the increase. When I first came to Wheaton the mean GPA was 2.6. A decade later it's up to 3.0. The administration is concerned that the faculty hold the line against this trend lest grades on a transcript be rendered meaningless. When I turned in final grades last term the registrar noted with praise that one person flunked and two received Ds. Is the lady a sadist who secretly hates college kids? Not at all. She was merely reflecting the pressure we all feel to maintain quality standards.

So I'm caught in the middle. I feel an internal struggle between Em as the good-guy friend and Em as the hard-nosed prof. If I let myself be pulled toward the side of leniency I hear squawks from the administration. When I ignore the extenuating circumstances that contribute to poor performance, students cry foul. I've somehow betrayed our closeness. When you're responsible to more than one clientele, conflict is likely.

The Eye of the Beholder

Last night I sat with my daughter in front of the TV and watched the Miss Universe contest. Believe it or not I found something more interesting than the swimsuit competition. Although the live audience was kept in the dark, each judge's score was flashed on the screen for home viewers. I was amazed at their lack of taste. Girls who lacked grace or charm were selected as finalists. Beautiful women were passed over completely. It made me wonder if the results were predetermined. Was it fixed? But then Sharon and I began to compare notes. We couldn't agree either. We had the same standards of attractiveness, we were looking at the same people, we just perceived each contestant differently.

The truth of the statement hit me. Beauty is in the eye of the beholder.

Different perceptions of the same event can cause conflict. I think this happens with my tests. I tend to ask short-answer questions. If you were in my class you might get a question over the first part of this chapter that ran something like this: "I suggest in my chapter on conflict that there are some positive aspects to group conflict. Cite three such benefits. Answer in a few words or phrases." Many would cry, "It's just another example of the grocery-list test Em gives. Boy, is he nit-picky!" I'd hear their comments and scratch my head in frustration. To me the item is getting at the central point of the first two pages. Two people of good will can look at the same thing but register different impressions.

Different Goals

"Why do we have to take a test anyway?" It's a good question. I hear it often. My first answer isn't popular. I have exams to goad students to do the course reading. I'm excited about the assignments I make. I spend lots of time and effort trying to find articles that present meaty ideas in a readable style. When I discover one, I want students to read it. All of us have great intentions, but we all tend to slough off unless someone holds us accountable. The fact that the line in the library is longer on the eve of an exam suggests the necessity of quizzing.

I also want to differentiate the good students from the poor ones. I'm not particularly enamored with the grading system, but given the fact that I have to turn in marks at the end of the term, I want to give As to the students who get more out of the material. Most tests distinguish the lousy students from the rest, but don't help determine the ones doing topnotch work. When the average is eighty-five out of a hundred, everyone can agree that a forty shows poor performance. But how about a ninety? Should I give the gal who got a ninety an A while the guy at eighty-five gets a B? The difference between them is slight, yet

I've got to figure out some way to dole out these scarce resources. So I write a tough test that has an average grade of sixty or seventy. That way I can differentiate the outstanding from the merely competent.

My students naturally want to show me what they've learned. That may sound like what I've written above, but it's not necessarily the same. I want to discover what they haven't learned. That can get discouraging to them, because part of what they've learned is on the feeling level rather than factual material.

It's one thing to be able to define deviancy. It's quite another to feel the sting of rejection reserved for the nonconformist. But I don't know how to assign a grade for emotional discovery. It'd be like grading kissing. So I've stuck to measures of head knowledge, realizing that they may have little to do with what a person really learned. The oft-heard statement "This test didn't give me a chance to show what I got from the course" highlights the problem. Our different aims cause conflict.

Values at Variance

Values are the traffic lights of our life. For most of us the toughest decisions are not between good and bad, but between two goods or the lesser of two evils on the down side. Take freedom and equality, for example. If we can't have both, most of us would pick freedom as the more crucial of the two. Yet that's a question of priorities. Not everyone in the world would rank the two in that order. We often don't even stop to consider that there's choice involved. Values are the deep-seated oughts that dictate the choices we make. In a conflict of values we don't see the other person as merely misguided. He's morally wrong.

I think I spot two questions of value in the classroom strife over my testing. The first has to do with the value of hard work. Effort *ought* to be rewarded. The Protestant ethic runs deep in my students. The fact that a class member has spent ten hours studying for an exam is a prima facie case establishing his or her right to an A. Anything less wouldn't be fair.

My expectations are different. Whoever claimed that we lived in a just world? God is just. But there are great inequalities in life. I wish there weren't. Yet some students can skim the assignment and gain a complete mastery of the material. Others have to spend hours poring over the books to gain a bare working knowledge of the stuff. The difference in world views sets us up for conflict that runs deeper than the wording of a test question.

The second question of value is cognitive style. In the literature this is known as holistic thinking vs. dichotomistic thinking. I choose to refer to these two types of people as lumpers and dividers. Lumpers seek to capture the big picture. Dividers want to break down an overwhelming problem into bite-sized components. They think the whole equals the sum of its parts, and they want to analyze each part in a logical order. When it comes to testing, lumpers are most satisfied with an integrative essay. But, as you've probably figured out by now, I'm a divider. I write my tests with short-answer items designed to focus on single issues. That's great if there's a cognitive fit between us. Very frustrating when there isn't.

Personality Clash

I've saved personality clash for last because I don't think it explains very much. Most will say conflict is caused by a clash between two people who can't get along. But *why* can't they get along? I think the first five causes I've listed cover most of it—power struggle, contrasting perceptions, competing roles, separate aims and differing values. They are also the reasons we feel someone rubs us the wrong way. So personality may be simply a catch-all term to describe the flash points of a relationship. Having said that, it's still possible there's an X factor that causes people to click or clash.

I react strongly against large, pushy women. (A psychiatrist might note that for most of my childhood years I was dominated by a fat, bossy, older sister.) I see red when a girl fitting that description approaches me   talk about a test. I tune out her words and prepare myself for emotional battle. This isn't exactly a mature reaction, but we're talking about what is rather than what ought to be. Conversely, I'm a sucker for a pretty face. I melt before a diminutive girl with a soft voice. Guys get a more neutral reaction from me. I suppose these could be called personality factors, as could impatience, prejudice or sheer cussedness. But I think of these as the result of other conflict-inducing causes rather than as originating forces. Besides, saying that a guy's stubborn does nothing to handle the conflict. It merely suggests that nothing short of death will solve the impasse. So I won't deal with personality as a serious cause of conflict.

When you take a look at the other causes I've listed, you'll note a pattern. Every one of them deals with differences—differences in position, perception or outlook. This gives us a clue as to how successful leaders might manage conflict within their groups. The key would seem to be to ignore, minimize, remove, resolve or surmount the differences that confront the group. That's not a single strategy. Each one calls for a different leadership skill. In the rest of the chapter we'll look at five different ways of dealing with conflict. Let me say before we start that I'm not committed to any one of them as *the* way to go. They all make sense in some situations. I tend to favor the final method I'll present, but leaders shouldn't cut themselves off from a full arsenal of stratagems.

Avoidance

One way of dealing with conflict is to avoid it. Whenever it rears its ugly head, change the subject. An old Navy man told me that there were three *verboten* topics on ship—sex, politics and religion. (Doesn't leave much room for significant discussion, does it?) Apparently this was the captain's way to guarantee amicable relations.

Avoidance can take two forms. One is to stay clear of any topic that will stir dissent. As the old Chinese proverb says, "Never wake a sleeping tiger." The other is to withdraw from the group when things get heated. Better to duck out before the tornado hits and flattens everything in its path.

Some students have chosen this route. They told me they wanted to take my course but heard how tough it was. They needed a high GPA to get into grad school, so they skipped an Em Griffin class. But even if a student enrolls, avoidance is still an option. Some oversleep on exam days with amazing regularity. Others drop the course just before the midterm. Still others take the test, do poorly, but never voice their frustration. On the inside they're dying, but they will not face me openly with the issue.

I'm no stranger to avoidance. I sometimes arrange my tests for days I'll be off campus! While this makes scheduling sense, saving valuable class time for lecture and discussion, it also helps me avoid the inevitable flak. I hand tests back at the end of the hour and announce that I'd be glad to talk to anyone about the quiz—in my office at another time. They can tell there's only a grudging willingness on my part, so the stratagem weeds out all but the most vigorous objections. Before the semester begins I may anticipate the fire I'll draw by giving a test and end up substituting a paper, journal assignment or other less reactive measure. That's avoidance.

Strategic withdrawal can make sense in some instances. Why stick around and get clobbered if you know it's coming? Tolerating or ignoring differences may be wise when the issues are trivial. And when you're ready to explode, avoidance is a way of counting to ten. So prudence sometimes dictates that we back away from confrontation. But avoidance is a lousy pattern to fall into.

Leaders who shun dissent see differences as eternal, inevitable, written in stone. They react to all conflict as if it were sin—an evil which will produce schism in the midst of believers. I don't buy that, and neither does Scripture. In Ephesians 4 Paul says, "Be angry but do not sin." This suggests that conflict and sin are not synonymous. It's possible to differ with passion without offending God. He goes on to urge, "Don't let the sun go down on your anger." I know of only two ways to follow that advice. One is to do the Joshua bit and keep the sun from setting while the war rages inside. (Good luck!) The other is to get your anger out where you and others can deal with it. Unfortunately, most Christians are loath to do this. They'd rather swallow their irritation. Of course that kind of feeling is hard to stomach, so the body keeps score. As with stifling self-disclosure, ulcers, headaches, high blood pressure, colitis and tight-lipped unloving saints result. There's got to be a better way.

Giving In

Perhaps the easiest way to reduce conflict is to yield to the other person's demands. My students don't like tests? O.K. I'll quit giving them. Or from their perspective, does Em think tests are important? So be it. We'll grin and bear it.

People who adopt this style of accommodation usually believe that differences with another are personal attacks that drive people apart. Conflict means rejection and therefore calls for personal sacrifice. I can purchase peace at the cost of ignoring my needs and desires. It's a high price to pay, but Christian love requires that I be willing to give up my wants for the sake of group harmony.

If you detect a trace of sarcasm in the last two paragraphs, you're right. I've known Christians who've given up their birthright to purchase a few moments of tranquility. That isn't to say that giving in is always wrong. There are times when it's eminently reasonable. If the person on the other side has all the clout, and you're bound to lose in a showdown, prudence suggests that you submit graciously. Sometimes the issue is crucial to the other person and trivial to you. In that case, why not let him have his way. You can also build up credit for the future by accommodating now. ("I let you have what you wanted before; now it's my turn.")

As a teacher or parent I might go along with what you want

144

even though I'm convinced you're wrong. I know that you'll benefit more from goofing up your way than doing it right my way. You need a chance to learn from your mistakes. And speaking of mistakes, as far-fetched as it may sound, it's just possible I might discover my cherished beliefs are in error. I hope I'll have enough integrity at that point to announce my discovery.

Giving in makes sense in all of these cases. But some folks try to smooth over every possible conflict. David Augsburger calls this sloppy agape.[2] They give up the courage of their convictions in order not to ruffle the relationship. It makes you wonder how solid the friendship is if it could be shattered by a touch of disagreement. And aren't some issues worth fighting for? There's a third approach to handling conflict.

Competing

If accommodation sacrifices principle to maintain the relationship, competing means a willingness to tube the relationship for the sake of convictions. There are times when this strategy makes sense.

Suppose you're dealing with a question of morals or supreme truth. Ducking the issue would be the act of a coward. Giving in would violate all that you stand for. Try persuasion. If that doesn't work, you may have to resort to force. There are times in life when we have to be willing to go to the mat for what we believe.

Forcing the issue seems like a legitimate act when time is short. Sometimes any decision is better than the imminent disaster which will befall if you don't do something. Should the people in a rubber raft caught in the quickening current as it approaches a waterfall try to reach the safety of the left bank or the right? There's no time to argue. Whoever has the power to make the judgment stick should make a command decision.

I'd also defend a combative style for some timid souls who have given in to others' demands all their lives. Whether from

"With our current hard feelings, would anyone object to my praying with my eyes open?"

genuine love or from a fear of rejection, they've consistently down played their own desires and let others have their way. Now they're tired of playing the doormat. They want to taste the heavy wine of self-worth, liking themselves enough to insist that they get their share at the banquet of life. I'm all for a feisty, competitive approach while they develop some assertive muscles to help them cope in a world of sharks.

The fellow who went to the dean about a pass/fail option chose a win/lose strategy. He won. But did he really? He built up lots of enmity with me in the process. He got his "pass" for a minimal amount of work, but I felt an edginess with him the rest of the quarter. That may be my own immaturity, but a competing style often generates bitterness. The Allies won a clear victory in World War 1. But the harsh Treaty of Versailles sowed the seeds of World War 2. That could happen to me. "Look, you crummy students, I'm the teacher here. If you don't like the way I run my class, get out. I spent four years of graduate work getting a Ph.D.,

146

and I've taught this course for ten years. No lousy sophomore is going to tell me how to write a test."

Of course I'd never use those words or present it in that mood and manner, but sometimes I've echoed those sentiments. A teacher's got big guns and lots of ammunition. It's tempting to use the power position to mow down the opposition. But of course it doesn't stifle dissent, it merely drives it underground where it can fester.

I think there's a certain personality that revels in competition. (I know I used to be this way.) I'm not talking about enjoying a friendly game of tennis, but rather the compulsive desire to win an argument just for the sake of winning. Jaw stuck out, eyes burning, all the issues are black and white, good or bad. Differences between people need to be erased through persuasion or force, and we know just the one to clean the slate. All in all, it doesn't appear to be a healthy approach to group leadership. I want a bit more flexibility and warmth in my mentors.

Compromise

Perhaps the best we can do is to get part of what we want. We could enter negotiations with the other side and come up with a solution that gives each of us a portion of what we desire. I could sit down with a committee of students and hammer out a compromise. I will give tests—four of them. And I will ask questions designed to pick up whether or not students have mastered the material. But I'll try to write it so that the mean is seventy-five rather than sixty. I'll include an integrative question that's one-third of the grade, and I'll hold a voluntary review session the night before each exam. It's not everything I could hope for, but I can live with it. So can the class.

This kind of bargaining is based on a spirit of cooperation. I'll probably never be best friends with my opponents. But I respect them as men and women of good will, and our negotiations will have left the door open for future relationships. It's the democratic way based on the belief that differences should be aired, that reason can prevail, and that there's a spot of humanness in those on the other side.

Compromise places an equal emphasis on your convictions and on your concern for a continuing relationship. You don't get everything you want, but life goes on amicably. You hope that the fruits of cooperating this time will make seeing eye to eye a bit easier the next. It makes sense under a number of circumstances. A balance of power is one of them. Often both sides have enough clout to frustrate the other but not enough to dictate a solution. When the issue is moderately important, when you care about the people, when you can't afford an impasse, compromise looks pretty good.

A nagging doubt remains, however, about adopting bargaining as our standard response to disagreement. When we begin with the premise that we need to split the difference, we know down deep that we aren't going to get everything we want. Have we given up too much? Is there a chance of resolving conflict completely satisfactorily without endangering our ties with others involved? It sounds too good to be true. But that's the possibility offered by our final method of handling conflict—carefronting.

Carefronting

The term *carefronting* was coined by David Augsburger to combine the best of both worlds: a loving care for the other person and an honest confronting of the differences that separate us.[3] Non-Christian theorists support the same concept, but use terms like *problem solving* or *collaboration*. People who enter into conflict situations with that kind of commitment see disagreements among people as natural, neither good nor bad. Differences are merely the occasion for creativity while demonstrating our solidarity with others. I use the term *commitment* advisedly. Successful carefronting doesn't happen by chance. It takes time, energy and willingness to break out of the narrow boxes in which we wall our lives. It's not for the faint of heart. I've plotted the five different methods of handling conflict on Figure 8.[4] The horizontal axis represents concern for the ideas in question. The higher the number, the greater the commitment to have a specific viewpoint accepted. The vertical axis represents concern for the relationship. The higher the number, the greater the commitment not to break fellowship over the issue. You can see that the carefronting approach is not willing to settle for half a loaf on either concern. Obviously you can't always pull that off, but I'll cite four different routes that I've used to attain the goal. It is do-able.

One is *role play*. Role play helps us see the world through the eyes of another. I did this with my class one time. All of us were feeling grumpy as we discussed the midterm. I asked for a volunteer to pretend they were me, and I tried to place myself in his shoes. We had no script or predetermined lines. We simply reacted as we thought the other one honestly would feel. I discovered how frustrating it was to prepare for hours and then be confronted by insignificant items that placed a premium on rote memory. He experienced the bind I feel to survey a cross section of the material, and yet not take hours of class time to give it.

What we came up with was a testing procedure whereby I would write ten integrative essay questions and pass them out ahead of time. Students would then know what was expected as they read. They could prepare with absolute certainty for the test, with an opportunity to present some in-depth knowledge, integration and application. I would select one question at random right before the exam. This meant the whole test could be written in thirty minutes and graded in a reasonable amount of time. Since they wouldn't know ahead of time which item would pop up, they'd have to read all the material. I was happy, he was happy, and the class bought into the solution. If we had compromised both sides would have had to give up part of what they wanted. This way everybody got their full desires while placing a high value on the relationship. That's carefronting.

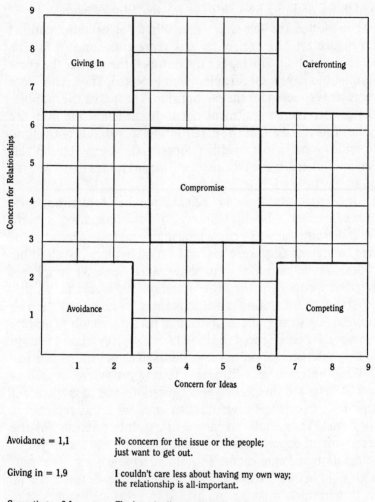

| | | Avoidance = 1,1 | No concern for the issue or the people; just want to get out. |

Avoidance = 1,1   No concern for the issue or the people; just want to get out.

Giving in = 1,9   I couldn't care less about having my own way; the relationship is all-important.

Competing = 9,1   The issue is all-consuming, but I don't give a hoot about how others feel about me.

Compromise = 5,5   Both the problem and the people are moderately important to me.

Carefronting = 9,9   The issue is crucial, but so is the relationship. I'm not willing to sacrifice either.

Figure 8

150

Role play takes a certain amount of vulnerability. You know ahead of time that you won't be able to view the world solely from your perspective when you're through. Yet if both people have a 9,9 commitment, they'll toss themselves into the effort. Status differences go out the window. That's part of its power.

There's a less dramatic way to accomplish the same results. Both parties commit themselves to an *empathic dialogue.* Sharon presents her feelings. Before Jill can respond she has to restate what Sharon has said in different words. Not until Sharon says, "Yes, you've got it. That's what I'm saying," can Jill broach her viewpoint. Then Sharon has to abide by the same ground rules before she can respond to Jill.

I've seen it take up to ten minutes for one person to really catch what the other has said. Some observers have noted wryly that the technique works because everyone gets so tired they finally give in. But that's not the case. Carefronting means finding a position where both parties get what they want. Empathic dialogue can aid that process because it helps build shared perceptions. We start seeing things through the same pair of glasses.

A third approach to carefronting involves *third-party counsel,* a third person with the best interests of both people at heart trying to bring warring factions together.

Right now I've taken on that function with two folks in a volunteer organization. One is a gal who's a close friend. The other is a very talented guy whom I respect. But they can't see each other for schmatz. (Don't try to look it up in the dictionary. It's my own term.) Their boss asked them to get together with me in hopes of staking out some common ground. It's not easy, but they're beginning to discover signs of humanity in each other.

I've been on the receiving end too. Jeanie and I have found it helpful to get together with friends and talk about our marriage—parenting, sharing the faith, work around the home, sex, recreation and so on. Our "counseling couple" listens in on the conversation, occasionally intervening with a question or comment. If we get hung up on some point, they can feed back

Drawing by Maslin; © 1981, The New Yorker Magazine, Inc.

"Mr. Kenny here will attempt to resolve our differences."

what they see happening from their neutral vantage point. It helps to have referees in the wings in case things get sticky. Then we do the same for them. It draws us all closer together.

Couldn't the same thing be accomplished with just the two of us? Not necessarily. There's a lawyer's maxim that states, "The attorney who represents himself has a fool for a client." The same can be true in intragroup conflict. It's nice to have a friend in court.

The *search for a supraordinate goal* is a fourth way of collaborating. (Almost sounds like a Sci Fi movie, doesn't it?) A supraordinate quest is one in which an overriding need makes lesser goals seem unimportant. People pull together in time of war. Freak weather disasters draw folks together. A tornado or two feet of snow can cause people to close ranks more effectively than a sermon or public appeals. And when my wife got cancer the petty hassles over missed phone messages and overdone meat soon disappeared. You don't sweat the small stuff when facing the Big C.

You certainly wouldn't want to court war, flood or pestilence just to lessen conflict within your group. But often people could rally round a common goal if one was articulated. I see that as a function of leadership. The good leader has the knack of spotting the deep desires of his people and appealing to the highest motives. "Ask not what your country can do for you, but ask what you can do for your country" was not just an effective political slogan. It was the clarion call of John Kennedy that ultimately launched the Peace Corps.

I'm not sure my class and I have ever come upon a common goal that made grading seem trivial—although our joint disgust with a school calendar that scheduled classes on December 23 came close. But we've been able to agree that our ultimate class-room aim is wisdom, and this has set off a fruitful discussion as to what that means. Some of our conclusions:

☐ All truth is God's truth.

☐ Unexamined raw experience is not education.

☐ Emotional learning is just as important as head knowledge.

☐ None of us like the grading system.

Our common appreciation of wisdom as the ultimate goal freed us to explore points of agreement.

My final suggestion for carefronting is quite simple. *Fight fair.* This is the advice of George Bach, a conflict specialist who claims that there's nothing wrong with a good interpersonal fight.[5] Like popping a blister or lancing a boil, a healthy sparring session with eight-ounce gloves can relieve pressure that's infected the relationship. It can be an exhilarating workout, one that develops muscle tone and ends with the combatants respecting each other's ability. Making up after the fight is nice too. The problem comes if one or both of the boxers don't fight fair. Bach has developed an elaborate Marquis-of-Queensbury-type list of rules to insure that nobody gives a rabbit punch or hits below the belt. Here are a few of the guidelines that I've found helpful in keeping conflict productive:

1. Admit you're mad. Don't pretend that you agree with every-one else or that you feel comfortable with the group when you

"We deal with it by talking about it."

don't. This may sound risky, but it's really safer than letting the anger fester. That's gunny sacking. You toss all the slights, hurts and irritations into a bag until it's stuffed full. Then you clobber them with it. It's overkill, like dropping an H-bomb on Luxembourg. Dealing with complaints as they occur makes more sense and is biblical as well. In 1 Corinthians 13 Paul reminds us that love doesn't keep account of evil. By keeping short books, getting out our anger before the sun goes down, we'll avoid an eruption.

2. Own your anger. It's tempting to place the blame on the other guy. "You make me mad" is a typical and nonprofitable charge. "I make me mad" is heard rarely, but more accurately describes the situation. It's *my* anger. Dealing with it is *my* problem. Letting our language reflect this reality can help. Usually "I" messages move us further toward solving the problem than "you" messages. It's the difference between being assertive and aggressive. When I say, "I want . . . ," I'm presenting

my desires up front. When I say, "You must . . . ," I'm aggressively demanding the other to do what I want. The normal reaction is "Oh, yeah?" "So's your old man!" Or "Who died and made you king?" Taking responsibility for our own feelings is a quantum leap toward carefronting.

3. Avoid sarcasm. Nothing torpedoes an honest attempt to carefront like a caustic quip. Lashing out in anger is at least honest and straightforward. No one can doubt that you're ticked. But sarcasm gets in a furtive dig. If the target objects, you can just shrug your shoulders and say, "I was only joking. Don't be so touchy," thereby righteously getting in a sneaky second jab. As I read Scripture, Christian sadism is not an option. So sarcasm is out.

4. One beef, and one beefee at a time. We have an infinite capacity to cloud the issue by bringing in extraneous data. If a student complains that I tested on material that wasn't assigned, I'm liable to come back with a charge that he ducked the real issue on his last term paper. The rejoinder is nothing but a smoke screen to get me off the hook. It so complicates the issue that Solomon himself couldn't sort it out. Hence, one complainer with a single complaint works best. After we've wrestled that one through we can move on to the next arena or a different opponent. Tag team matches are only for show, not serious fighting.

Do I fight fair with my students? I'm not sure. I try. It's tempting to use my status as the prof to put down complaints in a backhand manner. I know there have been times when I've used cutting humor to embarrass students in front of their classmates. I repent of doing that. It's not just. I'm committed to hassling out differences in a just manner, to fight fairly.

In this chapter I've suggested that conflict is not all bad. We started by taking a brief look at some of its causes. Common to all of them was the idea that differences cause discord. Each of the five methods of handling those differences makes sense in some cases. Admittedly, however, I put my thumb on the carefronting side of the scale when it comes to adopting a habitual style of conflict resolution.

I do so with a bit of fear and trembling. My present students know only too well that the tension continues. But perhaps that's not a bad note to end on. Conflict is not something we can take care of once and for all. It takes constant management. In that sense the leader is a bit like a lion tamer in a circus. All that pent-up fury in the big cat is what makes life interesting. Handle it right and you put on a terrific show. But turn your eyes aside for too long and you may get mauled. It's the nature of the beast. Ignore it to your peril.

Part Four

Influence
in
Groups

8

Persuasion

We met the train at 3:00 Sunday afternoon. I went in my official capacity as president of MCF, the University of Michigan chapter of Inter-Varsity Christian Fellowship. Joyce, our vice president, was with me. We'd received word that our new IVCF field rep would visit our group that night. We were told to pick her up at the Ann Arbor train station and spend time with her until the meeting. We were a bit apprehensive. Our executive board was used to flying solo. We hadn't seen a staff person for six months and weren't sure exactly what it was we were supposed to do with "our leader" until seven o'clock. It turned out that our vague unease was well founded.

As she stepped off the train she announced: "My name is Lynn Jones. Please call me Lynn." But we read her mood and manner as saying, "I'm ready to give you the counsel and advice you've been needing this past year." We took her to the student union for coffee. She told us that she felt Christians shouldn't purchase anything on Sunday so she'd pass, but to feel free if we wanted some. As we sat down at the table she leveled me with an intense gaze and asked, "How's your quiet time?" It was a long four hours.

Lynn meant well. She took her job as devotional adviser quite seriously. Perhaps that was part of the problem. In the process she took herself too seriously. Our spiritual well-being was vitally important to her. I think we would rather have felt that she cared about us.

It would be easy to read these paragraphs and conclude that I see any attempt to persuade group members as misguided, foolish or wrong. Not so. I've opened this chapter with the story of Lynn because it contains three themes that help introduce the legitimate attempts of leaders to persuade their people. The first is the theme of devotional life with God. Three different people have had an impact on my quiet time with Christ—each through a different type of influence—compliance, identification, internalization.[1] Interestingly enough, all of these folks have had touch with Inter-Varsity. So this will be the second thread that binds the chapter together. Finally there's the question of ethics. You can tell that Lynn's attempts to move us left a bad taste in my mouth. It goes beyond that, however. There are moral responsibilities a leader must consider when he or she sets out to persuade. These often get cheated in a morally bankrupt secular world. But for Christians they've got to come first. In the next few pages I'll lay an ethical foundation that I think can make us part of the solution rather than part of the problem.

The Ethics of Influence

I believe we have two ethical responsibilities: to really love the people we're trying to affect and to be just in the way we treat them. Love and justice. Easy to say; hard to do. I'll start with love.

Elsewhere I've listed six types of false lovers that illustrate immoral attempts at influence.[2] A friend of mine took the idea and came up with the following series of drawings. They illus-

Reid Victorsen

The Nonlover

trate better than I can what it means to be an unethical lover/ leader.

Nonlovers are leaders who refuse to lead. They have something of value to share with their people, but decline to make the effort to share it. Perhaps it's a basic shyness, a fear of failure or a

Reid Victorsen

The Legalistic Lover

lack of conviction, but from the other end of the telescope it looks suspiciously like they don't care about them.

Legalistic Lovers have a set image of what people should do and be. They are more concerned that people live up to standards than for their individual welfare. Their actions have the form of love, but not the substance. They take the obligations of leadership seriously, but their actions spring from a sense of duty rather than the passion of human warmth.

Flirts play with love. Flirtatious leaders have no deep commitment to the group. They are more interested in quick conquests. Once they get people to see things their way, they drop them flat. They are off on the chase for new blood.

Seducers are tricky as they seek to gain an advantage. Any method which makes their viewpoint seem attractive is fair game. Access to power, promises of friendship, fake stories that impress—all are part of the seductive leader's repertoire.

Rapists use force to have their way. Rape is frighteningly easy for leaders. They can use their power to compel members to buy their version of truth; and they can drive away a nonconformist. Psychological force is equally immoral. When we try to make a

The Flirt

Reid Victorsen

The Seducer

person comply by laying on guilt, or use our position to publicly embarrass a deviant, it's an act of rape.

Smother Lovers can't take no for an answer. They see disagreement as a personal rebuff, so they heap on incentives to insure compliance. Persistence can be a virtue. But smotherers

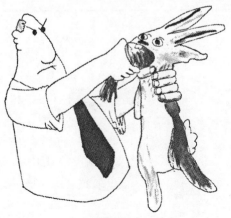

Reid Victorsen

The Rapist

163

Reid Victorsen

The Smother Lover

operate out of a need for approval rather than out of love for the folks they are trying to convince.

True Lovers care. It's been easy to parody the sins of false leaders. It's much tougher to present a clear picture of loving influence. I can do no better than the self-portrait sketched by Paul as he reminds the Thessalonians of his love.

Reid Victorsen

The True Lover

Our attitude among you was one of tenderness, rather like that of a devoted nurse among her babies. Because we loved you, it was a joy to us to give you not only the gospel of God but our very hearts—so dear did you become to us.... You are witnesses, as is God himself, that our life among you believers was honest, straightforward and above criticism. You will remember how we dealt with each one of you personally, like a father with his own children, stimulating your faith and courage and giving you instruction. (1 Thess 2:7-8, 10-12 Phillips)

That passage is a good jumping-off point for the second requirement of ethical behavior: justice. Paul speaks of actions that are honest and straightforward. It's not just enough to feel warm vibrations toward others. Justice requires certain deeds regardless of how we feel about people.

Just behavior means not imposing our beliefs or standards upon all of our followers. The key word is *imposing*. We may try to influence; in fact we should. But these attempts at persuasion must always leave inviolate another's free right to choose.

I picture ethical leadership as the process of giving people the opportunity to cloak themselves in my ideas. I can wrap them in an attractive package, present it personally and even request that people open it in my presence. But they themselves must unfold the garment and try it on for size. Unfolding vs. Imposing.[3] It's the difference between offering another something precious and strong-arming them into a straitjacket. I'd like to pursue this distinction.

The Golden Rule states, "Do unto others as you would have them do unto you." Strict adherence to these words would help us steer clear of ethical hot water. We'd regard our partner as the very one we are. In doing violence to another I'd be hurting myself. There's a problem however. I'm judging what the other person wants by my own feelings. I assume everyone else in the world is like me. 'Taint so!

I'm a touch-oriented person. I love a backrub. The way to this man's heart is not through his stomach; it's through a warm hug. If I slavishly apply the Golden Rule, I will go around hugging everybody. Problem: Not everyone wants to be hugged—at least not by Em Griffin. To be truly ethical I'm going to have to see things through their eyes rather than my own. This has lead some to suggest a Platinum Rule: "Do unto others as they would want you to do unto them."

This rule implies dialogue and lots of it. I've got to discover where they are and what they want. This will take much time, talk and trust. A dialogical ethic therefore suggests that the same persuasive attempt could be moral when directed toward one person but unjust when laid on another. Is this relativism masquerading as ethics? No. There are biblical obligations that reign supreme regardless of what either party wants. Thou shalt not commit adultery is a moral duty to be obeyed even in the face of overwhelming mutual desire. But not all ethical choices are that clear. The Bible is silent on many moral dilemmas. It's here that the dialogical ethic of the Platinum Rule comes into play.

Although relativism is an empty charge, there are two legitimate objections to the Platinum approach. The first concerns our own standards. What if the other wants you to beat them with a whip but you don't happen to be into sadomasochism? In fact you have strong moral scruples against it! The "do what they want you to do" approach compels you to ignore what you know is right. The second drawback is one of sheer energy. The Platinum Rule is an exhausting standard. It puts you at the mercy of every follower's whim. You've got to respond to their desires no matter how unreasonable. We can knock down both of those objections by restating the rule in terms of a prohibition. "Do not do unto others what they don't want done to themselves." This standard of justice preserves the integrity of both parties, and it lets you get enough rest and relaxation so that you can gear up for another day of leadership.

Love and justice. That's what a leader has to be concerned with when he tries to influence group members. Some feel that these are basically the same thing, that justice is merely love distributed equally. But I see them as distinct. Suppose for instance I try to persuade my group of college students to avoid the draft. Love requires that I be concerned for their well-being. What are the consequences of draft resistance? Will they go to jail, be outcasts in society, avoid being killed? In short, is this good for them? Justice asks different questions. Am I breaking the rules, avoiding duties or violating their rights as I seek to influence them to be pacifists? Justice has to do with obligations.

Lynn Jones's visit to the Michigan IVCF group had problems on both counts. We felt that she didn't really care about us as people. That's unloving. We also felt that she violated our privacy with her probing questions. That's unjust. Were we being too hard on her? Perhaps. But I see a tremendous responsibility on Christian leaders to do what's good (love) and what's right (justice). As Buber puts it, "One cannot divide one's life between an actual relationship to God and an inactual I-It relationship to the world—praying to God in truth and utilizing the world. Whoever knows the world as something to be utilized knows God the same way."[4]

With this ethical backdrop, I'll now present three methods of influence. See which one is appropriate for you and your group. It would be easy to figure that we've paid the necessary lip service to ethical considerations, and now rub our hands together in anticipation of getting down to important practical matters. Don't do it. The issues of good and bad, right and wrong, are questions that need to be raised again and again when dealing with leader influence.

Identification

I became a Christian through the influence of a girl named Ruth. She wasn't the designated leader of our young people's group. As a matter of fact, I was! But in terms of real influence, Ruth had the clout. It's been said that there are four classes of group members:

1. Those who make things happen.
2. Those who watch things happen.
3. Those who have things happen to them.
4. Those who don't even know things are happening.

Ruth was in the first category. She was attractive, vivacious, with a contagious enthusiasm for God. For most of us, high school is a time of cliques, trying to be part of the in crowd and avoiding the jerks. But Ruth moved from group to group with ease. To her, everybody was a good friend.

I was in the fourth category—at least spiritually. Although I was elected president of the youth group, I had no knowledge of the Lord. The only time I'd ever opened our family Bible was to press my biology leaf collection. It was the biggest book on the shelf. If someone had asked me if I was a Christian I would have looked at him or her quizzically and said, "Sure. I try to be a nice guy." But it wasn't an issue. No one asked.

I dated Ruth once or twice at the end of my junior year. It was all very casual, just some good times together. But I wanted it to be more. At the beginning of our senior year she suggested we go together on a weekend retreat. "We'll have lots of time to do some serious talking," she suggested. My mind was flooded with images of us lying back against a Lake Michigan sand dune, gazing at the stars, our heads together in deep conversation. "I'm for it," I said.

Surprise! The serious talking we did was about Jesus Christ. Ruth assumed I was a Christian and wanted to help me draw closer to the Lord. She gave me the Inter-Varsity pamphlet *Quiet Time.* As we went through it together she showed her excitement that God not only allows us to pray to him, but that he actually desires it. She encouraged me to block out some time each morning to read the Bible and pray. So I did, just as simple as that. And I became a Christ-one in the process.

I obviously wasn't convinced so much by what Ruth said as by who she was. I was attracted to her and wanted to have a relationship that would go beyond the weekend. I hung on to her every word, the result being that I heard a lot about Jesus. Did I believe what I heard? Yes, but that wasn't the motive for entering the faith. The impetus came from my desire to be close to Ruth.

It may strike you that identification isn't the most noble of reasons for changing your whole life around. And yet it's often where the action is. Not just in guy-gal relationships but among same-sex friends as well. Paul reminds the Thessalonians that they became followers of him and through him, Jesus Christ (1 Thess 1:6).

A few things have to happen for identification to produce lasting change. You need a persuader who's viewed as attractive and desirable. There's no absolute standard. It's all in the eye of the beholder. The more winsome the source, the greater the pull of identification. Second, the one to be influenced has to define himself or herself in relationship to the attractive person. Sometimes it's a total desire to be just like one's hero—the star-struck little leaguer modeling his every action on Pete Rose, including the way he combs his hair Other times it's a reciprocal role (lover, employee, disciple, daughter) where the influenced party tries to live up to the other's expectations. Either way she or he has got to know what's wanted. Finally, the attractive source will hold sway only as long as the relationship is important to the admirer.

John Stewart has a helpful way of picturing relationships as "spiritual children."[5] As you and I get to know each other our spiritual child is born. If we draw close in friendship, our spiritual child grows to maturity. If we ignore each other, our child remains stunted. Stewart claims it's impossible to kill our spiritual child as long as one of us remains alive. But neglect can cause atrophy, and hurt can maim. Using this imagery, a leader's influence ceases when a member abandons his or her spiritual child. It continues on, however, when the offspring is tended and nurtured.

Note that Ruth didn't even know how greatly she affected me. It was only weeks later, when I told her, that she realized the impact she'd had. That's typical of change that occurs through a process of identification. It appears to happen in an offhand manner. In fact, leaders who set out to build up their attractiveness often do the opposite. We don't react kindly toward those who seek to impress us.

I recently shared a platform with a homiletics teacher at a preaching workshop. He deplored the lack of ministerial eloquence. He exhorted his hearers to become larger than life in the pulpit. "Don't let your own personality or failings creep into your message. Remember you are God's man. You must create an impression of strength." It was probably the worst advice I've heard all year! When it comes to identification, vulnerability is a strength.

For two years my son and his best friend were discipled by our youth pastor, a charismatic guy with everything going for him. It was a clear case of identification. They even called themselves Hench #1 and Hench #2. The term was short for henchmen and aptly described the relationship. Whatever Gary said, it was O.K. with Jim and Scott. The guys picked up some reflected glory because all the other kids knew that they were favored ones. I've tried to figure out what it was about Gary that made him such an attractive figure to the whole community. He was a good athlete, had a great sense of humor, spent gobs of time with kids and was a good speaker. Yet somehow that didn't explain the depth of passion my boy felt for Gary. Finally another parent nailed it down. "Gary's not a cardboard cut-out. He's real. He burps and scratches." Maybe leadership-training courses should give lessons on being human.

Identification poses two problems for leaders. The first is that folks may have trouble getting past the person to the issue at hand. The admirer swallows the point of view whole because it was given by someone admired. But opinions need to be chewed and digested if they're going to affect the body. Unless leaders make a point of encouraging folks to question, probe and even doubt their opinions, that vital nourishment may be lost.

The second problem is ethical. When the leader is irresistibly attractive, persuasion through identification is seductive. Sören Kierkegaard tells a parable of a prince who falls in love with a peasant maiden.[6] He thinks to bring her to the castle so that he can woo her. Plan B is to go to her humble cottage accompanied by his chariots, soldiers and horses. But he realizes that neither course would be fair. How could she help but be dazzled by the princely splendor. So he resolves to cast off all royal advantage, dons the garb of a poor woodsman and proceeds to her home to plead his cause.

The great Dane presents this story as an analogy of Christ stripping off his prerogatives as God, coming to earth as a mere mortal so that we wouldn't be roped into the kingdom of God without an honest chance to say no. Attractive leaders may be held in such high esteem that their idle musing is instantly accepted as gospel truth. It's not a power most of us have, but I've seen it happen once or twice.

"If you love me, you will keep my commandments," says our Lord (Jn 14:15). That's a pure case of trying to persuade through identification. We've seen that it's a rather simple, straightforward approach to influence. Other methods are different but also effective.

Compliance

I wish I could say that I remained constant in my prayer life after becoming a Christian. The first year I faithfully blocked out fifteen minutes each morning to read Scripture and talk to God. But when I went away to college I got much more sporadic. At first I actually spent more time with the Lord. Fifteen minutes was too brief to grapple with the Word and pray fervently. Yet I was like the third soil in the parable of the sower. The seed had taken root, but trouble and persecution choked it out. Perhaps the term *persecution* is a bit strong. I did, however, have fraternity brothers mock my faith, and everyone including myself was uneasy at my half-hearted efforts at sharing Jesus Christ.

Things reached a low point when a friend came into my room unannounced and caught me in the act of reading my Bible. I quickly answered him that I was reading it for my course in great literature. As a prayer warrior, I felt like a draft dodger.

I was still a firm believer. I was just totally bankrupt in the spiritual disciplines of prayer, Bible reading and witness. ("What else is left?" you ask. I actually did pretty well in the areas of generosity, service to the brethren and basic joy in living— things high in the fruit of the Spirit pecking order. I've since grown a bit suspicious of equating devotion to God with a single Christian virtue.) I came face to face with my problem at the end of my sophomore year.

I've always had a rather high need to exert influence. That's one reason why I'm writing this book. Anyway, I decided that I wanted to be president of the Michigan Christian Fellowship. I craftily noticed that the two previous head officers had attended an Inter-Varsity camp in the summer. For this reason I decided that I'd go to the Campus-in-the-Woods, a remote camp on an island a few hours north of Toronto. But the camp schedule called for a forty-five-minute quiet time every morning before breakfast. I thought I'd go nuts.

I'm an activist. Given my spiritual state, there were a number of things I'd rather have done than sit on a rock and pray. Swim around the island, play volleyball, repair the door on our cabin, read a novel, write my girlfriend, talk with people, canoe— almost anything was preferable to silent meditation. But there was a strong pietistic emphasis the whole month. The main speaker stressed that God was more interested in who we are than in what we do. While everyone else nodded solemnly, my every nerve fiber shouted no.

It soon became obvious that I wasn't playing the game. The camp director took me aside and made the following offer: "Em, I notice that you aren't taking advantage of our scheduled quiet time. I'll make a deal with you. You want to speak when we go off the island to conduct church services in Bracebridge. If you'll settle down each morning like everyone else, I'll let you give the children's sermon next week and the sermon the following Sunday. This is just between us. I'll want to know where you'll be each morning, and I'll check up on you. But this is your chance to try your wings as a speaker. How 'bout it?"

I was hooked. I wanted to speak in those services so bad I could taste it. So I dutifully climbed up on a rock and read Scripture for a half an hour. I then shut my eyes to pray for the final fifteen minutes. Once or twice I'd hear the director tiptoe past.

Surprisingly it turned out not to be an empty pharisaical practice. Despite my lousy initial attitude, I got a lot out of what I read. I was intrigued by Christ's encounters with people, his teachings, his miracles. My prayers became more balanced. Besides a list of requests, I began to praise God for who he was and confess to him who I was. So all in all it worked. The director got what he wanted and I got what I wanted. (Incidentally, I did a super job.)

What I've described is a pure case of compliance. To make it work the leader has to have control over something the group member wants. It can be a teacher with grades to give, an employer with money or a pastor with the promise of a church office. The desired reward is conditional on proper performance.

Many of us are uncomfortable with this type of behavior exchange. We see it as nothing less than a bribe. But what really sticks in our craw is the blatant nature of the transaction. We wouldn't be so bothered if it were done in a more subtle manner.

Each term I ask students in my persuasion course to enlist a new donor to give a pint of blood. Ideally a person could be recruited by an altruistic appeal. "Think of the life that might be saved by your contribution." As a practical matter, most students resort to compliance. All sorts of incentives are offered. Chocolate-chip cookies are high on the list, though back rubs, typing services and cash are not unknown. I once overheard the conclusion of a successful transaction. "So it's agreed," a girl in my class said to a guy. "You give a pint of blood this afternoon,

*"I'm not kidding around anymore, Mrs. Whitman. You have our book.
We have your son."*

and I'll go out with you tonight."

Personally I don't have any trouble with compliance as a persuasive technique as long as the behaviors are ethical, both parties openly agree and there's a parity of power between them. This last condition does not always hold. I was in the Philippine Islands and had a chance to talk with peasant farmers who had once owned their own land. They were poor but self-sufficient. Along came the big pineapple and banana multinational corporations and offered to buy the land. The price wasn't fair, but the promise of more cash than they'd ever held before was irresistible. They were out their land and soon out of work. To me this was an example of unjust pressure to comply. As leaders we often operate from a position of privilege. Anytime we make an offer that can't be refused, we've violated our people's freedom of choice. But barring this abuse, compliance seems ethically neutral.

Another potential problem with compliance is that it may touch the body but not the soul. There were a number of days that I just pretended to read the Word. Once I even put my Bible cover around a paperback novel. I gave outward compliance to the director's will, but there was no inward conviction that this was really the way to go.

Surveillance is another problem. Persuasion lasts only as long as the guy with the goodies is monitoring our performance. "I've got to watch him like a hawk" is the lament of many supervisors who operate by compliance. Once the director went off the island for two days. While the cat was away, the mouse didn't have a quiet time.

I have a final problem with using compliance as a habitual style of influence. It can turn us into hypocrites. There's a place for merit badges, brownie points and cash bonuses. But self-fulfilling prophecy holds sway. Treat me like a kid long enough, and I'll start acting like one. If you're convinced I'll only be moved by continually dangling baubles in front of my face, I'll be glad to oblige. But we need a way to have influence that will last even after the enforcer is gone. There is such an animal, and it's called internalization.

Internalization

Twenty years passed between my college experience with Inter-Varsity and when the Fellowship significantly touched my life again. In many ways I was the same person—an activist who continued to find it easier to talk to someone about Jesus than get down on my knees and pray to him. There were some significant differences, however. I no longer wanted to get to the top of the organizational mountain just because it was there. People had become more important than programs or power. I also had what I considered a second conversion experience, a new insight into the kingdom of God. I became convinced that our Lord had a special identification with the poor, the hungry, the oppressed, the hurting. It was this conviction that led me to attend Washington 80, an Inter-Varsity-sponsored convention dealing with the concerns of the city.

I came to Washington 80 with my own agenda. I knew God wanted me to get involved with the plight of the poor, but I was struggling to figure out how to serve without falling into the trap of paternalism. I had an even greater need. The demands of teaching, family life, friendships, writing, competitive sports, church responsibilities and speaking had brought me to the point of emotional burnout. I wanted some relief. With these needs very much in the front of my life, I was influenced by Bill Leslie.

Bill is the pastor of LaSalle Street Church in Chicago. It's an inner-city congregation on the edge of the infamous Cabrini Green housing project to the west. To the immediate east is Chicago's Gold Coast. Some of the high-rise condominiums sell for a million dollars. To the dismay of some church-growth theorists, Bill has fashioned a polyglot mixture of wealthy professional people, struggling students, poor Blacks and suburban folks with a heart for the city into a unified Christian force for justice. It's a church with a social conscience. Programs include teen-age recreation, evangelism, discipling, tutoring, an emergency food pantry, care for the shut-in elderly, job training and searching, legal aid services and aid for unwed mothers. The most ambitious project has been the creation of new housing in a burned out section of the city. Atrium Village is Chicago's showplace of mixed housing where rich and poor, Black and White can rent attractive apartments on a sliding scale according to their ability to pay. All of these services are offered not only in the name of Jesus Christ but in a spirit of love that has brought many to the Savior. You can see why Inter-Varsity brought Bill to Washington to lead a seminar.

I sat in on Bill's session. It was good. He laid a biblical foundation for identification with the poor. A verse from Jeremiah stood out in particular. Referring to King Josiah, the prophet declares: "He pled the cause of the afflicted and needy; Then it was well. Is not that what it means to know Me? Declares the LORD" (Jer 22: 16 NASB). He then gave lots of practical tips on how an upper-middle-class suburbanite could aid an urban slum dweller without coming on like the great White Bwana dispersing trinkets to the natives in the mud huts. After the seminar I sought Bill out and said I'd like to get together to talk.

We met twice within the next day and a half. We cut out of a general session that night and talked for two hours. The last morning we had breakfast together and sat at the table so long after eating that the waitress offered us a luncheon menu. Most of the time I talked and Bill listened. I shared the changes that God had begun to work in me. Although I started with an account of my journey toward helping the poor and hurting, Bill's sensitive ear soon picked up the fact that I was hurting too. The hectic pace of life was beginning to take its toll. Our second time together Bill shared his own tendency to overschedule, overextend and be overwhelmed by the pressures upon him. He suggested that the only way he could survive was through periodic times of concentrated prayer and meditation. He also stressed that social action unaccompanied by inner worship would quickly degenerate in him to an empty do-goodism. Times of contemplation were necessary as a wellspring of power.

I was impressed! But I figured that this was a special gift he had. We agreed that we had the start of what could be a budding friendship and vowed to get together along with our wives when we got back to Chicago.

The exhausting work pattern didn't let up when I returned. If anything I was dashing from one thing to another more than ever. It was a month before the Leslies and the Griffins could mesh their schedules. During the interim I thought a lot about what Bill had said. I picked up a book on the spiritual disciplines of prayer, meditation and fasting. I was intrigued by the spiritual depths promised to the believer who pursued these means of grace. I was ready to give it a try.

When we finally got together as couples I pumped Bill for advice on the specific route to go. He recommended blocking out a day or so for a personal retreat. While it would be possible to do this on my own, perhaps I'd find it helpful to have some direction. I agreed, not knowing exactly where he was going.

He knew of a Catholic conference center where you could book in for odd lengths of time. In fact it was less than ten miles from my home. I could make a thirty-six-hour silent retreat without the interruptions of phones, upcoming appointments or classroom responsibilities. He suggested the name of a nun there whose vocation was spiritual direction. If I contacted Sister Anne, he was sure she'd take it from there.

Wow! That was radical stuff for this plain vanilla Protestant boy. I had visions of cloistered cells, swinging incense and repeated "Hail Marys." Bill didn't push it. He just gave me the center's phone number and suggested I consider the possibility. I took his advice—length of time, place, spiritual director and all.

It turned out to be a turning point in my prayer life. For the first time I was able to meditate on a verse of Scripture and listen for that still small voice of God. Instead of flooding heaven with a bunch of junk mail, I learned under Sister Anne's direction to concentrate on a single attribute of God and taste that for a long period of time. I came away edified and refreshed. I will do it again without Bill's urging. More importantly, I've incorporated some of the meditation techniques into my daily quiet time. That's internalization.

The first thing to notice about the process is that it's made me a true believer. This is different from compliance where internal conviction doesn't match outward behavior or from identification where the belief is more in the person than the idea. Nor is continued belief or action dependent on Bill Leslie hovering over my shoulder to check up on me. I could never see Bill again yet still hold true to the new spiritual discipline. Obviously this is the kind of influence leaders would like to have. In the pecking order of persuasion, compliance is at the bottom. It borders on the raw use of power and takes continual use of resources and energy to maintain. Identification is a good step up, but is dependent upon the desire for a relationship. Internalization is the home run of influence. It's the ultimate aim of sensitive Christian leaders. The person *really* believes. Like a tree planted by the river, he shall not be moved (Jer 17:8).

How does it work? First, it takes credible leaders. They need some recognizable expertise so that their words will have the ring of truth. That was Bill. He'd won my respect by the quality of his deeds. The next requirement is that the person being changed has to have some specific needs or desires. I desperately wanted to be effective in serving the poor. Equally important, *I* wanted to get off my high-speed treadmill. By being a good listener, he was able to spot these desires. He then tied his advice into my overriding values. Even though his solution was outside my previous experience, I was hooked.

In chapter two I referred to leaders as change agents. It's an awkward term, but we don't need to shy away from the idea. Unless you see yourself as a mere co-ordinator, at least part of your job as a leader involves persuasion. You've got to select a strategy of influence. From the members' perspective, compliance doesn't look too great. Sure, they get something they want, but their actions are in no way linked to their conviction. The hand bone ain't connected to the head bone. They could easily turn bitter or cynical if they go through motions they don't believe in. It's not wrong per se to try to induce compliance. After all, it may be the only option open to the leader who hasn't had the opportunity to develop friendship with his group. But it would be wrong to stay there. Why grub around with irrelevant payoffs when a lasting relationship or inner values beckon?

Can action taken through compliance turn into identification or internalization? Sure. This happened to me when I took an Integration of Faith and Learning seminar at my college. I didn't want to spend those idyllic summer weeks with my nose in the books, but the trustees of the school decreed that it was a necessary part of getting tenure. So there I was. Sheer compliance. The leader of the seminar was an exciting scholar. I was attracted by his quest for learning, his encyclopedic knowledge, his ability to ask penetrating questions. I wanted to please him, to look good in his eyes. Compliance gave way to identification.

My topic was ethics of communication. As I got into the subject matter I forged a defensible ethical position. I felt a growing urge to translate this ivory-tower theory into a moral stance that would grab people. It became an obsession. The last two weeks I'd sit down to eat with a book in my lap. The discussion of love and justice at the start of this chapter grew out of that seminar. Identification with the instructor was no longer the issue. I wanted to do it because I thought it was worth doing.

The conversion of my motivation to a higher plane happened because I had some freedom within the requirements of the seminar. Suppose the leader had put together a lock-step assignment. I would have done what was demanded to get tenure, but moaned and groaned the whole way. He gave me some wiggle room, however, and it made all the difference.

At the start of the chapter we saw that freedom of choice was central to ethical influence. Now we see that the same freedom will stimulate internalization. I find it comforting that in God's plan what is most ethical is also most effective.

180

9

Deviance

Deviance is a bad word. To be deviant is to be different, odd, strange, queer, peculiar, uncooperative, wrong. It's particularly hard for leaders to tolerate deviance. Any show of independence is seen as a personal attack on your effectiveness. And when it's a Christian group, there's a strong temptation to label it sin.

I've had a chance to examine deviance at the two-week island course in group dynamics. Certain patterns seem to happen the same way almost every year. The way leaders emerge is one such regularity, discussed in chapter three. The creation of deviants is another.

The last sentence is not a misprint. I've used the term *creation* because it best describes the surprising process I've seen. Each winter I select eight students from a large batch of applicants. I attempt to get folks with a variety of personalities, backgrounds and interests. I also try to make sure that the students I pick will work hard at living together, and are up for a certain degree of sharing and self-disclosure. It wouldn't be fair to place someone with severe emotional problems into this intensive group experience, so I work at screening out potential misfits. In short, to the best of my knowledge, we start without a deviant. Yet by the time the course is half over, he or she is there in living color.

How does this happen? More importantly, what's the best way for leaders to deal with this part of group life? I'll present my conclusions in a series of questions and answers illustrated by my island experience. Your group may be quite different in nature, but think twice before dismissing what I've discovered. Each answer is consistent with research findings in the study of deviant behavior.

Question: What kind of person is a deviant?

Answer: There is no one type. Deviancy isn't a personality trait. It's a label conferred by the group upon those who act differently.[1]

Learning this came slowly. The second year I spotted the group singling out a gal as "shy" because she rarely spoke up, especially about herself. I chalked it up as bad selection on my part and vowed to make sure that the next time I would get highly verbal students who were willing to be open. Yet I felt a vague unease because I clearly recalled our precourse interview in which she expressed her eagerness to share on a personal level. The following year it was a fellow who took three showers a day. This had no small effect on the group because we ran the generator only five hours a day and hot water was at a premium. The guy was quickly tabbed as a "cleanliness nut." I could spot no similarity between the girl who carefully metered her words and the fellow who was lavish in his use of water.

In succeeding years the class included the Honda Freak (a fellow who would rather ride a trail bike around the island than eat or sleep), the Screamer (a girl who would yell in your ear at

"Why didn't you guys tell me you were getting expensive gifts?"

the least provocation) and the Competitor (a guy who would study half the night with a flashlight suspended over his head so he could beat everyone on the morning quiz).

All of these individuals felt genuinely grieved that the group considered them weird. To them they were acting naturally. In fact, most of the things highlighted by the island group as eccentric were considered normal behavior in their home fellowship. There was nothing particularly perverse in their island behavior. They were just different. Different = deviant. I've since discovered that some of my "normal" high self-disclosers from the first course were regarded as "running-off-at-the-mouth egotists" back on campus. Deviancy is in the eye of the beholder. If you act in a manner counter to others around you, you're a deviant by definition. Therefore, I find it helpful to regard nonconformity not as an act of personal cussedness but as a clash between two subcultures.

Conforming the Deviant

Question: How do groups react toward their deviants?

Answer: They feel threatened and they try to change them to make them conform.[2]

You'd think that one lousy dissenter wouldn't bother the majority. Not so. The mere presence of one who doesn't adopt the party line is a threat. There's always the possibility that the cancer will grow and topple the established order. But even if that seems far-fetched, the close proximity of a variant viewpoint forces people to reconsider what they thought was a universally accepted idea. Suddenly the world's not quite so safe, and that's uncomfortable.

We play lots of games after class at the island course. Soccer and volleyball get most of the action during the day. Darts, Boggle, Clue, charades and chess are featured at night. One year a rather noncompetitive chap named Steve announced that he'd just as soon pass on game playing. Now there was no law that said you *had* to participate. It wasn't a stated objective of the course. But the group automatically assumed that everyone would take part. This is typical of many group expectations. The strongest ones are those which are unwritten. They don't need to be formalized because their truth "goes without saying."

Steve's nonparticipation had a chilling effect on the others. They saw his decision as some sort of judgment on the sheer fun of playing. To Steve it was no big deal, but the others had a tough time abandoning themselves in a game of charades when they knew that he wasn't willing to lose his cool. The positive value of competition was called into question too.

As a result the group tried all sorts of ploys to persuade Steve to change his mind. The teams were uneven; everyone needs a study break; one girl offered a back rub; one guy threatened him with sand in his bed. All of these were said with a smile, but the kids left no doubt that their intent was serious. This pressure was heightened by the fact that Steve wanted to be

"Eleven hamburgers, one frank. Eleven coffees, one tea. Eleven apple pies, one chocolate cake...."

part of the group. It would have been a different story if he couldn't care less. Pressure to conform can only be as strong as a person's attraction to the group.[3]

Steve's nonconformity stimulated lots of communication in his direction. The number of messages aimed at him increased when he showed signs of wavering. I don't recall what finally won him over. Perhaps it was the offer of a back rub. (That would have done me in.) But as his resistance faded, so did most of the communication. It was sad in a way, and I think that there is a lesson here for Christian leaders.

We have a natural tendency to lavish attention on those outside the fold. They expect this interest to continue if they enter the fellowship. But unfortunately we usually neglect the folks after they've adopted the standards of the group.[4] These are the unethical tactics of the flirtatious lover described in the last chapter. An awareness of this pattern can insulate us against that tendency.

Question: What if the deviant refuses to cave into the majority desire?

Answer: At that point others in the group begin to reconsider their position and even entertain the possibility that the deviant's behavior or attitude is O.K.[5]

Marv was a political radical. He expressed a blatant suspicion of any human authority. One night I put down one of his pet beliefs. I cloaked my judgment in the full garb of academic certainty. "As one who has a Ph.D. in the field of persuasion, Marv, I must say you're wrong." It was a dumb thing for me to do, and he reacted immediately by giving me the finger—an obscene gesture of derision. The group gave a sudden gasp. Lewd nonverbal behavior might be O.K. in some secular circles, but the others left no doubt that this form of disrespect was out of bounds in our Christian group. They were more bothered by Marv's action than I was.

I liked Marv a lot and felt that his quick response was at least partially justified by the heavy-handed way I'd come down on his ideas. But the group's reaction was the strongest condemnation of deviant behavior that I've ever seen on the island. For the next twenty-four hours the other seven tried to convince Marv to apologize. But he'd have none of it. There aren't many radical students at Wheaton. He'd had lots of practice defending his position in the past and held firm in this case. As he told one girl: "The fact that Em is the prof doesn't make him God. He lashed out at me pompously, and my response was an appropriate way to deflate his puffed-up manner."

The group didn't buy Marv's argument—at least not right away. Publicly they held to the position that Marv was wrong. But their private journals began to express tentative doubts. By the end of the course some were openly questioning the fact that things were valid just because I said so. Undoubtedly this shift was made easier by my attitude toward Marv. But there's also no question that deviants who stand their ground can influence the group.

The effect of the sole holdout may be greater in the long run than the pressure to conform coming from a group. Majority influence usually affects immediate outward behavior. I tend to be a Coke-aholic. I love the stuff. A year ago I was tossed together with about five other people who thought Coke was sin in a bottle. The sugar would rot my teeth, the caffeine was addictive, the cost was exorbitant and the political tactics of the multinational Coca-Cola Bottling Company were immoral. I laid off the stuff just to avoid the hassle while we were together. But inwardly I still thought it was O.K. to drink Coke and felt a deep yen for its sweet taste.

Pressure to conform rarely touches inner conviction.[6] The lone stand of a deviant can. I recently met a girl who won't drink Coke. In the face of her resistance to the urgings of my friends and me, I now have to deal with the issue. My internal wrestling may not lead to immediate change, but later on a new attitude may percolate into consciousness. If it does, it will be an internalized belief, not mere outward compliance to the majority view. (This has in fact happened. I wrote this chapter a year before publication. For the last six months I've quit Cokes cold turkey.)

Question: If deviants won't give in to the majority will, and the group is unmoved by their attempts to sway them, what happens?

Answer: The group rejects the deviant.[7]

It's a simple answer for a complex question, but that's what happens. Sometimes rejection means actual ouster from the group. Fired, excommunicated, expelled. That would be rugged at the island. I suppose ultimate rejection would involve placing the offending party on a raft and casting it adrift. But there are lots of ways of rejecting people without removing them bodily.

The shy girl was assigned the dirtiest jobs. Since she didn't speak up, she suffered in silence. The cleanliness nut became the butt of many jokes. One time during dinner a fellow snuck away and hid all the soap and turned the water off at the pump. The would-be showerer's postdinner frustration was met with great amusement.

The group's attempts to reject the Honda Freak were thwarted at every turn. They served a meal just after he hit the trail. But

Cartoon by Robert Ross. Appeared in Saturday Review, *1975*

"We understand you tore the little tag off your mattress."

he didn't care if he missed dinner. He'd rather speed than feed. They compared test grades in order to put him down for lack of study. It had no effect. The following fall the majority was still working at showing their displeasure. Somehow no one remembered to invite him to the reunion dinner. A last minute phone call went unanswered and his absence was vaguely regarded as his own fault.

It was impossible to ignore the Competitor, so the group took to passive resistance. They removed the batteries from the flashlights, refused to reveal their own test scores and literally yawned in his face when he started boasting about his achievements.

Of all the abnormal behaviors I've mentioned, the antics of the Screamer were hardest to take. Her piercing shriek delivered twelve inches from the ear easily defeated two Extra-Strength Tylenol. It called for extreme measures, so she was sent to Coventry. That's an old-fashioned term for not talking to someone—pretending that they aren't there. This did nothing to reduce the number of screams, but after repeated attempts to get her to cease and desist, it seemed the only way to handle the revolting habit. When it came time to head home in different vehicles, it was not by accident that the groupings were four, four and one.

These responses may strike you as cruel. They are! There's nothing particularly Christian about rejection. But it's been my aim to paint a picture of the *is* rather than the *ought*. I'm not a fatalist. I think Christian leaders can break this cycle of rejection. I'll outline my views on handling deviancy in the final section of the chapter. But for now it's important to realize the facts of group life. Groups tend to reject people who insist on being different.

Question: How do deviants feel about their stature as outcasts?

Answer: They don't like it and they take whatever steps they can to avoid the displeasure of the majority.[8]

Deviants aren't dumb. Just because they're different doesn't mean they're stupid. They soon pick up the displeasure of the majority. The normals take pains to announce it. Less than twenty-five years ago Jim Crow laws in the South publicly branded deviancy by color as inferior. As late as 1970 an old San Francisco law remained on the books that made it illegal for a person with a deformity to be seen in public—something

I'm sure disabled Vietnam vets appreciated. Recently a popular song proclaimed that short people have no reason to live. No doubt many would accommodate to the norms if they could. But they can't. Hue of skin, amputation and smallness are givens. So the deviants try to mask their differences. Bleaching creams, artificial limbs and elevator shoes are about the best they can do.

Keeping a low profile is another way of avoiding group displeasure. They can't get mad at what they don't notice. This may actually involve walking on the other side of the street. More often than not it means standing mute.

There's a story about a backwoods boy who was drafted into the army. His small country church held an all-night prayer vigil just before he left for basic training. While laying on their hands, they prayed earnestly for a consistent witness that he wouldn't lose his faith when exposed to the ungodly guys in the military. When he came home on his first furlough they eagerly sought out how it was going. "Things are just great," he said. "I've been in the army for six months and nobody's found out yet that I'm a Christian."

In a small group setting the deviant opinion often goes unspoken. Loners hold their piece for the sake of peace but privately hang on to their attitude like a bull dog. So no one wins! The group is hurt by both the loss of stimulating ideas and the subtle resistance of one who they thought was with them.

Occasionally those on the edge of society will use a frontal approach. Instead of camouflaging their deviances, they'll come out of the closet and glory in their difference. Of course the gay liberation movement comes to mind. But homosexuals aren't the only ones to use the strategy. Since the day of Pentecost the "peculiar people" of God have banded together to proclaim their differences to a hostile world. Inter-Varsity chapters on a university campus are a case in point. Christian deviants—let's face it, that's what we are—come together and get positive strokes from other deviants rather than trying to get their approval from a secular majority.

Over long periods of time deviants have learned that they can expect better treatment from other deviants than they can from the mainstream—even if they aren't all different in the same way. For decades the Democratic party thrived on Roosevelt's grand alliance—separate minority groups who huddled together for warmth. Blacks, Jews, Catholics, immigrants and eggheads came together to counter the sting of the WASP majority. There seems to be an affinity among those who feel oppressed, whatever the reason.[9]

You may have noticed that I haven't used any examples from the island course to illustrate ways deviants avoid detection. Perhaps they've been so successful that I haven't spotted them. But in most cases the whole setup of the course systematically rules out that option. People are selected for their willingness to confront each other. We live together intimately for two weeks, daily discussing what's going on among us. The small size of the group doesn't facilitate pockets of resistance. The deviant stands alone. If someone *will* be different, he or she has to take the consequences. Of course this doesn't mean the person has to like it.

The Benefits of Deviance

Question: Does deviancy hurt the group?

Answer: No. A little bit of deviance helps a group get where it wants to go![10]

We've now come full circle. You'll recall that I claimed in answer to the first question that groups create deviants. That's surprising since the collective body works so hard to make the deviants love it or leave it. And it's obvious that all of this is no fun for the outcast. Yet despite the pain to all concerned, groups continue to foster and nurture deviance. It's almost as if an unseen hand prompts the group to single out one from their midst to fill the slot because one is needed.

Deviance is a necessary group role just as much as leadership. Without it a group will flounder. The first island course I ran contained no deviant. I was worried about potential conflict that might split our group, so I made sure that I picked responsible, loving, cheerful, positive people who abhorred discord. All minor irritations were smoothed over. For the whole two weeks there never was heard a discouraging word. Everything was upbeat, cooperative, nicey-nicey. And very little was accomplished.

Cartoon by Malcolm Hancock. Reprinted from Saturday Review

"Clifford, you're a very stupid elephant."

Our problem was that no one was ever quite sure what was acceptable and what was out-of-bounds. The uncertainty made people edgy. The oughts and should-nots of group life are largely unwritten. It takes someone who's willing to push the limits before folks know just how far they can go. Once the deviant arouses the ire of the group, everyone knows exactly how much liberty of movement there is without stepping over the line.

A deviant also gives meaning to the concept of reward. If nothing is forbidden, nothing is worthy of praise either. As TV westerns have shown, there are no good guys without the bad guys. Any attempt to systematically wipe out the bad guys leaves the group out of balance and desperately in need of a new villain. All this may sound silly, but it does happen.

Take for instance a small group of committed Christians. They desire to have a pure fellowship—to root out any evil within their midst. The only blight on their horizon is that one member feels comfortable going to R-rated movies—the kind with nudity and swearing. His deviance sets the standard of acceptable behavior. Self-censorship is seen as a good response to Philippians 4:8. "Finally, brethren, whatever is true, whatever is honorable, whatever is just, whatever is pure, whatever is lovely, whatever is gracious, if there is any excellence, if there is anything worthy of praise, think about these things." After failing to dissuade him from his lurid movies, the group expels him from their midst as one who is too loose. In essence they've pulled in the lines of moral behavior, but now no one is certain how far. Believe it or not, a new deviant will soon emerge from the hitherto "good" people. His or her O.K. behavior is now on the fringe and is the subject of condemnation. PG films are now suspect.

This splintering is typical of groups that want to purify their number. The group gets smaller and tighter but is doomed to always being dissatisfied as long as they insist on allowing no dissent.

Groups also need deviants for creativity. By its very definition, creativity is deviance. Henry is a pilot for a missionary aviation service. The organization has an understandable concern for safety and insists that everything be "done by the book." Any deviation from standard operating procedure is met with an immediate and harsh response from the pilot's supervisor. Henry was convinced that a given regulation about fuel management was dangerous. He rigged up a cross-flow gas line that provided a back-up safety feature. But of course it flew in the face of the mandate, which meant a "date with the man" to be chewed out. But what was seen as destructive deviance by his immediate superior, was viewed as blessed creativity by the organization's top management. Henry's "wrong" way of doing it is now standard operating procedure on all flights.

Similar things have occurred at the island. Most of the courses have had one distinct deviant. Their far-out ideas have led to commonly approved features of the course: two-meal days so we can have more time for recreation; a ten-minute evening break to watch the sun go down over the water; walks through the woods with Em so he can assess learning subjectively as well as by tests; a work day at the start of the class to bring people close together and so on. None of these ideas had been tried before.

They came from people who broke out of normal patterns of thought. If you won't color within the lines, you're a deviant. You may also be creative.

So groups need a deviant. But not two.[11] The only time the island course came apart at the seams was when we had two distinct deviants. The group tried to accommodate them both. But as they moved toward one they alienated the other and vice versa. So instead of coming together as a unified whole, we ended up with two subgroups of three, two isolates and lots of hard feelings. A larger group can handle two or more renegades, but a group of eight or less can only take one. But don't forget—they need one.

Question: In light of all this, what's the best way to deal with the deviant?

Answer: Since deviancy is a natural, healthy part of group life, sit back and enjoy it!

I know that's tough advice to follow. We often regard alternate views as a personal affront to our leadership. We're doing our best to run a well-oiled machine and we feel that an off-center gear will foul up the works. But that's where we err. People aren't cogs in a machine. They're unique human beings—and it's individuals that have rights, not groups.

No doubt there are occasional times when one fellow's nonconformity steps on other people's rights. The guy who stayed up half the night studying at the island is a case in point. He kept others from sleeping—and that's not fair. In a situation like that the leader has a duty to intervene in a way that won't embarrass. Going to a brother privately is the biblical route to follow. But those times are rare. Usually the group is best served by a leader who takes the stance of Voltaire. "I disapprove of what you say, but I will defend to the death your right to say it."

Try to heed the sage advice of Gamaliel. When the Sanhedrin was confronted by the disruptive behavior of the disciples he counseled, "My advice to you now therefore is to let these men alone; leave them to themselves. For if this teaching or movement is merely human it will collapse of its own accord. But if it should be from God you cannot defeat them, and you might actually find yourself to be fighting against God!" (Acts 5:38-39 Phillips).

Benign neglect was what he suggested. But since the Jewish leaders thought they had a corner on all wisdom, they couldn't tolerate deviance. And they ended up doing the very thing that Gamaliel warned against—opposing God.

I've always been impressed by leaders who don't feel they have a monopoly on the truth. They're secure enough to entertain different, even "wrong," ideas. The academic dean at my school once toyed with the idea of appointing a heresy committee. He wasn't advocating that the group try to root out unorthodox ideas. On the contrary, he was suggesting that it might be healthy for our Christian college to foster heretical thoughts—systematically encouraging folks to think the unthinkable. This goes beyond benign neglect. It tilts toward the actual care and nurture of the deviant.

The thoughtful leader's stance toward the deviant is like the octogenarian's view of old age. He was asked how it felt having yet another birthday to mark his advancing years. "Considering the alternative," he replied, "not bad at all." The alternative to deviance is not attractive either. Who wants to head up a mindless conformity? Sameness has a chilling effect on progress.

Sensitive leaders realize that stagnation would set in if they allowed it to be open season on deviants, so they use their position to eliminate unfair shots at those who are different.

As hard as this is, we have the comfort of knowing that our Lord lived—and died—with this approach to deviance. He was unable to see a crowd; every person was special. He knew them each by name. If he could put up with a political fanatic (Simon the Zealot), a pair of emotional hotheads nicknamed the Sons of Thunder (James and John), a man who openly questioned his resurrection (Thomas), a corrupt tax collector (Matthew) and a money grabber who betrayed him (Judas), how can we do less? In the long run it turned out to be a pretty good group.

195

10

Self-Fulfilling Prophecy

Hans was a clever horse. He and his owner astonished crowds with his ability as they toured the European continent at the turn of the century. Hans could answer any question:

How many Gospels are there?

What is the square root of 25?

How many letters are in the word Hippopotamus?

No question was too tough. As long as the answer could be indicated by tapping his hoof, he could handle it. Of course there were many skeptics. Some thought Hans had been programmed to paw out a certain sequence of numbers and that the questions were selected to fit the predetermined pattern. Others charged that the owner, Herr von Osten, was signaling Hans when to stop. So scholars from around the world gathered to put the horse to the test. They made up incredibly difficult questions. They removed Herr von Osten from the auditorium so that there was no possibility that he could control the animal. Even under these conditions clever Hans came through.

Then disaster struck. Someone asked Hans a question without knowing the right answer himself. In fact, no one in the hall was certain what the answer should be. Hans started pawing away his response to the question as usual, but after a minute it was clear something was wrong. As the crowd began to fidget, Hans's tapping became more tentative. He finally slowed down to the point where he stopped altogether, his hoof suspended uncertainly in midair. Slowly it dawned on folks that Hans didn't know the right answer either.

This discovery led to a whole new line of research. Scientists slowly concluded what they probably should have known all along. Hans couldn't add, subtract, multiply or divide. Neither could he spell. In fact there was no evidence that the animal could even understand the question. In that sense Hans was not clever at all. His owner was held up to public ridicule and the horse was put out to pasture.

What was the gimmick? How had Hans fooled the public for so many years? It turned out that the horse was simply an astute observer of nonverbal signals. If someone asked how many fingers human beings have, Hans would go into his pawing routine. As his hoof hit the ground for the tenth time, people would tense up in anticipation. Would Hans make a mistake? The horse reacted to the rising expectancy of the crowd and quit tapping. Actually he was quite clever. It just wasn't the ability that was advertised.[1]

The Power of Expectations

Expectations are powerful. Expectancy holds sway not only over dumb beasts, it affects humans as well. This fact of life has been labeled self-fulfilling prophecy. The mere expectation that an event will take place brings about its occurrence. When we look for something to happen in other people, it often does. How come? Why is expectation such a powerful force in our lives?

Two basic human needs provide an answer to this question. The first is the need to understand. The second is the need to make accurate predictions.

We all want to make sense out of the world around us. But it's hard because we're bombarded with conflicting data over the radio and TV and through the press and our personal contacts. We desperately desire to understand what's really going on out there. The hectic days surrounding the news of the 1978 Jonestown massacre in Guyana provide a good example. Every hour the newscaster announced an increased body count of those dying in the mass suicide. Reporters told us that Jim Jones had been a respected political force in San Francisco. Some compared the People's Temple to a Christian commune while others described it as a cult of Satan worship. I was stunned as the week progressed. I didn't know what to think or whom to believe. I wanted *Time* magazine to give the definitive interpretation of what had happened and what it meant.

Expectation is our internal authority. It makes order out of chaos. Just as an evening news anchorman edits and interprets the news, our expectation of other people helps us sort out conflicting impressions. But understanding the present is not enough. We also want to be able to forecast the future.

The ability to predict what's going to happen has cash value. No one is always accurate, but the person who can consistently call the shots on tomorrow's stock averages, weather or sporting events will receive a handsome reward. Why? Because knowledge of the future is power. This is equally true in interpersonal relations. If I know how you'll respond in a given situation, that puts me one up. I'm in control. You can see why I've made this chapter part of the influence section.

Because of their power and visibility, what leaders expect has a special impact on group members. If they think the group will do well, members will usually do their best to prove their leaders are right. If, however, they suspect that the group will fall flat on their collective rump, the group has a strange way of confirming their leaders' fears. Kurt Knight was a place kicker for Washington's pro football team, the Redskins. His field-goal percentage under the legendary Vince Lombardi was the best in the league. All that changed when George Allen took over as coach. For some reason Allen had little confidence in his kicker's ability. In the conference play-off game with Dallas, Allen had the choice of calling a close field-goal attempt or a play from scrimmage. Allen elected to run. When reporters asked why he hadn't called the obvious kick, Allen replied, "I didn't think Knight would make it." From that time on Knight's record went straight down.[2] The coach's expectation of failure turned into reality.

Whether the main thrust of the group is to complete a task, spur closeness or influence behavior, leaders need to mobilize the talents and energies of a diverse crew into a unified effort. It's like taking nine dogs for a walk at the same time, each canine pulling in a different direction. Most leaders want all the

"Those of you who came tonight expecting to see the performer work himself into a mad frenzy, tear off his clothes, and smash his instrument will be pleased beyond your wildest dreams."

help they can get. They look for the human equivalent of choke collars, whistles or dog biscuits to bring their charges to heel. What they don't realize is that people are more susceptible to a more subtle form of persuasion. We're all swayed by the expectations others have for us.

A Three-Step Process

As I'm writing this chapter I'm sitting in a college library wearing a pair of corduroy slacks, a turtleneck jersey, tweed sport jacket and Hush Puppies. Suppose I was dressed like this when we first met at your Sunday morning church service. You wouldn't merely shake my hand and pass by if you thought that you'd see me again. You'd try to draw some conclusions about what sort of person I am. You wouldn't have much to go on—my facial expression, tone of voice and rather casual dress. But that wouldn't keep you from making a host of assumptions which would guide you in our future times together.

Perhaps you'd conclude that I was a very comfortable and relaxed guy, and this would put you at ease. On the other hand you might assume that only a careless and disrespectful person would wear such informal clothes to a worship service. Either way you'd attribute personality characteristics to me that aren't inherent in my dress.

You have an active part in this. You're like a cooly analytic IBM operator who's running a computer search to compare my dress with other people you know. Or you're like a psychiatrist who's struggling to figure out my motives for wearing these clothes. A less flattering possibility is to view you as a self-deluded distorter of truth who bends perceptions to fit preconceived prejudices. In any case it's natural to make mental leaps based upon our expectations. We all do it.

The process usually goes something like this:

1. Perception. We see someone in action. It may be a man in a gray tweed sport jacket entering the church, a stranger smiling at us on a bus, a driver coasting through a stop sign or a woman patting her child on the head. Of course what we see may not be what actually happened. We're quite capable of filtering out some elements and injecting others. Expectation gets its first shot in the way it affects what we see and hear.

2. Judging intention. Once we've seen the man in the sport coat, the smile on the bus, the stop sign ignored or the parent and child, we immediately ask ourselves, "Did they mean to do it?" This concern is so automatic that it may not be conscious, but we still want to know. Was the action intentional or accidental? If we decide the act was unintentional, we tend to dismiss it from our mind. But usually we figure that folks are like the elephant in the Dr. Seuss story. "I meant what I said and I said what I meant," said Horton. And we expect no less. That's where expectancy gets its second crack.

3. Labeling. The girl on the bus is *friendly* because she smiled at me. The driver is *reckless* because he ran the stop sign. The mother is *loving* because she touched her child. There's an implicit assumption in each of these judgments that the action is typical and that we can count on similar behavior in the future. But it doesn't always work that way. The gal on the Greyhound may be a shrew, and the guy with the lead foot may in actuality be a compassionate doctor hurrying to an emergency. But we don't believe it. We attribute a personality trait to others on the basis of what we see. Our expectation can be stated bluntly, "People who act like that *are* like that."

What would you conclude about me based upon fleeting encounter? You could jump a number of different ways.

☐ Em is sloppy. He has no sense of what's appropriate.

☐ Em is casual. He's a relaxed guy.

☐ Em is poor. He can't afford a suit.

☐ Em is spiritual. He's here to worship God not show off.

☐ Em is _____. (Fill in the blank.)

Note that all of these labels involve a mental leap. They go beyond the bare facts of my attire. In fact, the adjective you pick may say as much about you as it does about me. In a sense, we are all amateur psychologists holding to our implicit personality theory. When we see a particular trait, like style of dress, we immediately call up all the other characteristics that are tied together in our mind with that trait and then label the whole batch.

This is when expectancy gets interesting. For when you label me sloppy, you encourage me to be just that, because once you conclude that I'm messy, you'll start treating me that way. It's not at all necessary that you announce your label to me. I'm quite capable of picking up your judgments through subtle nonverbal cues. And whether your label is flattering or negative, I'll slowly conform to your image. This is the self-fulfilling prophecy.

One of the most impressive demonstrations of self-fulfilling prophecy took place in an elementary classroom. An educational consultant gave children a new diagnostic test at the start of the year that supposedly showed which ones would have a sudden spurt of IQ. Twenty per cent of the students were labeled as late bloomers. In reality, of course, the test was a fake and the children were picked at random. But their teacher didn't know this. She thought they would actually do better than their class-mates. And they did!

The teacher never told them what was expected, but she didn't need to. By anticipating their success, giving that extra bit of encouragement, and spending a few additional minutes with them, she brought out the best in her special charges. The very act of labeling made it happen.[3]

It's not surprising that these children became the teacher's favorites. We all like those who perform well for us. But they gave their teacher the additional reward of living up to her expecta-tion. What was surprising, and a bit scary, is that those who had an unpredicted surge in IQ were viewed as bothersome trouble-makers. It seems that unanticipated success can be threatening. How do you react when you're expecting a person to be mean and he turns around and does you a good turn? The above re-search would warn that you might actually like him less.

Everyone has contrasting tendencies floating around inside: extrovert—shy, gloomy—optimistic, active—passive, scared—daring, logical—irrational, lazy—hard working and so on. There's always the possibility that either side can surface at any given time; and over time an individual probably acts both ways. So it's crucial which tendency we tickle with our expectations. If I point out your ignorance, you'll feel stupid and act dumb. If I catch you in the act of being intelligent, you'll feel clever and act wisely.

There's a tremendous persuasive power in labeling. We can nudge a person on to new ground by the labels we assign. This happened to me when I became a Christian in high school. I fell in with a group of Christian kids who assumed I shared their commitment to the Lord. They asked me to their Bible study, invited me to their parties, shared Scripture verses, and even selected me as an officer in their youth fellowship. They automatically expected that I'd be interested in the things of the Lord— so I was.

This had two significant advantages over traditional techniques of evangelism. First, I didn't have the feeling that someone was trying to change me. Therefore, I didn't throw up all of the defenses we usually do when we hear a TV ad, sales pitch or sermon. Rather I was relaxed and willing to hear what the others saw in me. Second, nobody told me I was a sinner. Standard persuasion theory says people must feel a need before they'll adapt your solution. First they itch, then you scratch. The church has often majored in making certain that people itch. Naturally many folks build up a strong resentment toward those spreading poison ivy. They don't stay around for the cure. If we focus on sin, they are liable to live up to our expectation.

Please don't think I'm soft on sin. But I think the full biblical witness is captured by the catechism response: "Man has the capacity for good but the propensity for evil." I came into the faith because some loving kids zeroed in on the redeemable side of Em Griffin.

This kind of positive labeling goes under many names— attribution, affirmation, stroking, giving warm fuzzies, accentuating the positive, building up. Whatever we call it, my experience suggests that we do it!

Psychologist Carl Rogers says that he finds it helpful to believe everything his clients tell him.[4] Other therapists would just laugh at this idea. They claim that their patients lie, evade and conceal the truth. They make it a practice to never take at face value what the patient says. But Rogers holds firm. He insists on labeling his clients as trustworthy. It's not that he's naive. He knows that they'll violate this trust at times. Yet he's discovered that unconditional positive regard is the most helpful thing he can offer the other person. It changes lives.

Of course labeling doesn't have much effect on a one-shot basis. Last week a woman called me an "insensitive S.O.B. who's always putting people down." This was heavy stuff that gave me cause to pause. Fortunately, however, a lot of other folks in the same group gave me feedback in the other direction, so I wasn't too shook by her outburst. But if I was labeled insensitive by a number of people, over a length of time, and in a variety of situations, I'd start thinking of myself in those terms. None of us is so sure who we are that we're immune to others' expectations.

We don't have complete knowledge of our attitudes or abilities. We constantly need others to help us define who we are. This is why we are so affected by others' expectations.You wouldn't think that this would be so. If *we* don't have a handle on our feelings and talents, how in the world can we expect others to have a clearer insight? I don't know. But it's a fact of life that we do.

Expectation doesn't work if it contradicts areas of self-knowledge we are sure of. This is why it's impossible to motivate someone else. Motivation has to come from within.

Motivating

We are the proud owners of a sad-looking basset hound. Yesterday our family sat on the floor to play cards. Bowser slowly ambled up and plopped himself down in our midst. He likes the warmth of human companionship and wanted to be where the action was. However, his presence smack in the center of the game brought the action to a halt. How to get him to move?

Repeated whumps on the rear end brought a soulful look of reproach and only grudging movement. He soon returned. My daughter, Sharon, suggested working on the other end. A bribe of

*"Looks like the pastor has found a way to motivate the
building committee."*

a graham cracker offered in the kitchen brought about a quicker response, but again he returned moments later to take his self-assigned place. By applying negative sanctions to his rump, or positive reinforcement to his mouth, I can get the hound to move. But movement is not motivation. We didn't motivate Bowser to leave. His subsequent return gives that idea the lie. His real motivation was to be with the rest of the family, and that desire came from within. Motivation can't be whipped up externally.

Many try. They offer all sorts of positive incentives in the hopes of increasing production. High wages, bonuses, stock options, shorter work weeks, health care, pension plans, background Muzak, impressive titles, keys to the executive john—all of these stimulate movement toward the goal. Momentarily. But when they become old the movement stops. The only real way to stimulate quality work is to make sure the work is stimulating. The leader's task is to structure the job so that it taps into the drives that are already present in group members.[5]

I'm fortunate to work under a dean and a department chairman who do just that. I love to teach. It's especially enjoyable for me to teach upperclassmen who are specifically interested in the things that turn me on—group dynamics, persuasion, interpersonal communication, ethics of influence. On top of that I have a strong desire to draw close to my students. I see some lifelong friendships ahead that began in the classroom. My dean and my chairman have stretched themselves to see that I've had the chance. Class offerings, scheduling, off-campus opportunities, film availability and total freedom of course content have enabled me to do what I wanted to do in the first place. Not only that, these two men continually let me know they appreciate the job I'm doing. What more could a guy want?

Lots. My office is a 6' x 10' cubbyhole, poorly lighted with absolutely no oral privacy. I see some of the administrative policies as a bit to the right of Attila the Hun, and no one's ever accused a prof at the school of being overpaid. But as long as my bosses structure the job so I can do what I'm driven to do, I won't be side-tracked by the small stuff.

People don't usually toss in their lot with a voluntary Christian organization because of the lure of money, comfort or prestige. They're already motivated. Give them something meaningful to do for the kingdom of God and watch them go.

What motivated people are looking for in a group is affirmation. They need to know that they are valuable members of the team. You say, "Sure, Em. But what if the guy is doing a lousy job? Which should I do, praise him or tell the truth?" My answer is both.

Take this book for example. I'd like to get lots of compliments on it. But I'm not so insecure that I want others to lie. What I really crave is honest praise. Suppose you are my editor who has the job to evaluate the writing halfway through the project. You'll probably see some good and some bad. I'd encourage you to expect it to be good, identify the parts that sing and let me know why they're so fine. "I like the creative use of examples. Your vulnerability is appealing. You are well-organized and easy to follow. And those cartoons are super." These positive strokes will encourage me to write even better. I'll be able to pick up what you didn't like by the absence of praise. The warm glow of appreciation will allow me to face the problem areas squarely. But first I need positive feedback. The good leader starts with the assumption that his people are going to do things right and then works creatively to catch them in the act of doing so.

The Pygmalion Effect

I began this chapter with the true story of Hans the clever horse. I'd like to finish with a fictional yet sensitive account of expectation at work. George Bernard Shaw's play *Pygmalion* is a beautiful example of self-fulfilling prophecy. Most of us are familiar with the musical version, *My Fair Lady*. In the play Professor Henry Higgins trains an ordinary cockney flower girl to talk and act like an upper-class lady. Although he's an insensitive, egotistical clod, Higgins is a master at languages. His crowning triumph comes when he passes her off as a princess at the grand ball. The girl, Eliza, has a different view of the process, however. While acknowledging the professor's skill, she credits the very real transformation in her life to the professor's friend, Colonel Pickering. In a touching scene at the end of the play she turns to Pickering and states the main point of this chapter better than I could—so I'll let her speak for me:

I owe so much to you that I should be very unhappy if you forget me. . . . It's not because you paid for my dresses. I know you are generous to everybody with money. But it was from you that I learnt really nice manners; and that is what makes one a lady, isn't it? You see it was so very difficult for me with the example of Professor Higgins always before me. I was brought up to be just like him, unable to control myself, and using bad language on the slightest provocation. And I should never have known that ladies and gentlemen didn't behave like that if you hadn't been there. . . . But do you know what began my real education? Your calling me Miss Doolittle that day when I first came to Wimpole Street. That was the beginning of self-respect for me. . . . Things that you showed me as if I were something better than a scullery-maid if she had been let into the drawing room. You never took off your boots in the dining room when I was there. . . . It made such a difference to me that you didn't do it. You see, really and truly, apart from the things anyone can pick up (the dressing and the proper way of speaking, and so on), the difference between a lady and a flower girl is not how she behaves, but how she's treated. I shall always be a flower girl to Professor Higgins, because he always treats me as a flower girl, and always will; but I know I can be a lady to you, because you always treat me as a lady, and always will.[6]

Part Five

A
Last
Look

11

Leadership:
A Personal
View

This final chapter will be a personal one. Over the last forty years I've had the chance to view group leadership close up from a number of angles. I think it all began when my kindergarten teacher asked me to lead the other kids down the hall to the gym because I was the only one who could tell time. (I know, it didn't make much sense to me either, but I was happy to get the honor so I didn't bother to ask.) Or perhaps it started earlier than that. For the first two years of my life my mother plopped me into a playpen so I wouldn't wander around. I saw leadership through the other end of the telescope. I'm told that my favorite song as a kid was "Don't Fence Me In."

I've been the president or chairman of a high-school youth group, a college Inter-Varsity chapter, the senior class at seminary, the Training Committee of the Young Life Board and a corporation which runs a ski resort. In other organizations I've had a supportive leadership role—student government in high school, board of deacons at church, faculty personnel committee at school. Often my role has been that of mentor or adviser—Young Life Club leader, swimming coach and my vocation as teacher. On occasions I've avoided a formal leadership role, preferring to work behind the scene—pastoral nominating committee, my son's hockey organization. As I think back over my history with groups, I realize that I've developed some rather strong feelings about leadership. My guess is that many of them have leaked out in the previous chapters. If so, fine. But I'd like to use this final chapter to share my biases overtly. Perhaps these musings are idiosyncratic (just once I've wanted to use that word) to me. But the eminent psychologist Carl Rogers claims that what is most personal is most general.

There's a rich treasure of leadership lore in Scripture. I've selected biblical leaders whose lives have struck me deeply. Perhaps my conclusions will resonate with you as well.

Closeness with a Few: Jesus
Typical organizational wisdom suggests that leaders hold themselves at a balanced distance from group members, because special bonds create jealousy among the others and make it difficult to direct the action of a friend. Our Lord ignored this advice. He had favorites.

Jesus was open to all comers. I know of no instance in Scripture where he turned folks away. Yet he picked twelve to be his special band, and spent half of his time with these. Further, out of the Twelve there were three who made up the inner circle: Peter, James and John. He chose them to be with him at the pinnacle of his glory on the Mount of Transfiguration, and he wanted them near at the depths of his despair in Gethsemane.

This caused problems. The disciples argued among themselves as to who would be closest to him in the kingdom. John insists on referring to himself as "the disciple whom Jesus loved." But consider the alternative. Intimacy is God's beautiful gift to his creation. If we hold ourselves aloof we aren't fully human. And how unwise to model a measured coolness when a spontaneous warmth could spread to the whole group.

The loneliness of leadership is very real. I find that I need closeness with at least one or two members to make it. Note that I said *need,* not just want, desire or would like. The island course I've referred to is a prime example. For two weeks I have a twenty-four-hour-a-day responsibility that weighs on me heavily. "What shall I teach tomorrow? Is the weather good enough to fly off for groceries? How can I keep Ruth from getting emotionally hurt again? Should I insist that they not eat on the couch? What if someone gets injured?" It's the decisions that kill me. I find that by the second week I've usually drawn close to one or two of the eight students. I don't plan it ahead of time. In fact sometimes I click with a guy or gal who initially turned me off. I try to keep myself open to all and let their response to me initiate the intimacy. But I need someone with whom I can bat around ideas, share and be myself. Some would say that's a weakness. For Jesus it was a strength.

Wanting to Lead: Isaiah

I said in the third chapter that I've never seen a true leadership draft. That has caused many Christians to go through all sorts of mental gymnastics. Down deep they want it, but somehow they feel the desire to lead is selfish, sinful. So they try to convince themselves that they didn't seek the office but the office sought them. Sophistry!

Paul told Timothy that anyone who aspired to the office of bishop desired something noble (1 Tim 3:1). Lest power cause his protégé to miss the point, Paul drives it home with a sledge hammer. "This saying is sure!" he insists.

I like the way Isaiah handled his call. The Lord gave Isaiah a vision of his majesty. Suitably awe-struck, the prophet-to-be was almost wiped out by his sin and inadequacy. God used an angel with a burning coal to assure Isaiah that he needn't be hampered by guilt. (Fortunately we don't need seared lips to gain that confidence. We have guaranteed forgiveness through Jesus Christ.) Then God puts the question out: "Whom shall I send, and who will go for us?" No hesitation, no false modesty for Isaiah. No mealy-mouthed protests about not really thinking he's capable, but if you insist. "Here I am! Send me," he shouts back. I'm sure that telling a stiff-necked people they were going to hell in a handcart had its moments. At those rough times I'd find it easier to go on knowing that I wasn't drafted. I volunteered.

Enthusiasm Covers a Multitude of Goofs: Peter

I like the blustery fisherman. He flubbed up *big*. I can identify with a man like that. He always said the wrong thing at the awkward moment. Some of his goofs are just funny. When Christ wanted to wash his feet he first refused, and then insisted on a bath. While still reeling from the impact of the transfigured Christ, he blurts out a silly suggestion about building some mini-temples on the hill. In a classic description, Mark states, "Peter said to Jesus. . . . For he did not know what to say" (9:5-6). And then there was the time he and the others were fishing after Jesus' death. When he sees a figure on the beach he lets out a whoop, "It's the Lord!" He then proceeds to put on his clothes and dive overboard. Most of us would have done it the other way around.

Other times his mistakes really hurt. He told Christ that he mustn't go to Jerusalem to die. Stung to the core, Jesus rebuked him, "Get behind me, Satan." He fell asleep in the Garden of Gethsemane. And then of course there was the big one. Under the miniscule pressure of a servant girl's gaze, he denied Jesus while his Lord watched on from the balcony.

Despite these faux pas he was the undisputed head of the growing band of believers. How come? Because Peter had a contagious enthusiasm for the Lord and his business. It was Peter who left his cash crop in the nets to follow Jesus. When Jesus asked them who he was, only Peter had the courage to stick out his neck with an answer. Seeing the Lord walking on water, Peter threw caution to the wind and stepped over the gunnel to join him. Standing before the same hostile Jewish leaders that condemned Christ to death, Peter boldly proclaimed, "Whether it is right in the sight of God to listen to you rather than to God, you must judge; for we cannot but speak of what we have seen and heard" (Acts 4:19-20).

Few will follow cautious, tight-lipped perfectionists who keep their emotions in check. But those with unabashed enthusiasm that spills all over can draw a crowd every day. If you have to err, err on the side of passion.

Don't Play God: Joseph

Who in their right mind would pretend to be God? It's seductively easy to fall into the trap. This is especially true for the Christian leader who's a good speaker.

For years I've spoken to high-school and college students about Christ. I've gotten pretty good at it. It's an exhilarating feeling to stand in front of a hundred youthful faces knowing that you've caught them with your words. The pretty girl gazes up raptly; the sincere young man nods in agreement. Heavy stuff! It's a short trip from speaking about Jesus to speaking confidently in the name of Jesus. And it's not much further from there to speaking as if I *were* the Master. My words are truth. Oppose me and you're opposing God.

Silly? I wish it were. But the history of the Christian church is full of leaders who got confused about who they were. Their followers don't help the cause by craving easy answers as much as the Israelites clamored for a golden calf. They promote their man to demigod status. Usually he doesn't resist too hard.

Joseph had problems playing God. He was aided by a doting father. He had administrative talents which catapulted him to the top from the bottom of a Canaanite pit. He also seemed to enjoy lording it over his brothers. His dream of them bowing down to him was not designed to win friends and influence people. But he got it right in the end. After Israel's death, Joseph's brothers groveled before him begging his forgiveness. It would have been tempting to encourage a bit of worship. But Joseph said, "Fear not, for am I in the place of God?" (Gen 50:19). The idea was as abhorrent then as it is today.

Every once in a while I hear talk about whether or not God is on our side. It usually comes during a war, sporting event or political campaign. As for me and my household, I'm more concerned that we be on God's side.

There are two kinds of people in this world—those who think there are two kinds of people in the world and those who don't. The first group sees everything in terms of black and white, the second can spot some grays. I want to be in the second camp. It keeps me from playing God!

The Strength of Vulnerability: Hosea

You may have noticed that the theme of vulnerability has permeated each section of the book. Sometimes I speak of openness and honesty, other times of taking risks or being willing to change. Whatever we call it, I'm for it. The opposite of vulnerability is impression management—the studied attempt to project an image. I'm against it. More than any other approach to leadership, vulnerability has served me well.

I was not always so disposed. In my early years I had a deep desire never to be wrong. This was surpassed only by my fear of being laughed at. These twin terrors naturally made me want to clam up. What others didn't know couldn't be used against me. I think the net effect on others was a vague respect, a definite uneasiness and lousy leadership. I couldn't be hurt, but I couldn't help much either.

I'm not sure what made me change. Perhaps it was the sheer weariness that comes from holding tight too long. No doubt exposure to a few great men who didn't feel the need of pretense freed me. But I began to experiment. I tried to admit my mixed motives, share my doubts and occasionally own up to shattered

"Write about me as I am, warts and all."

dreams. A funny thing happened. Rather than laugh at me, others wept with me. What I lost in impressiveness, I gained double in becoming approachable. I found that openness brought a warmth to my leadership style that was vastly superior to the practice of saving face. It was more fun too.

Hosea didn't have a choice. The Lord commanded the prophet to marry a prostitute. Everyone in town knew that Gomer was a harlot and a marriage license didn't affect her basic predisposition. Hosea was rejected by his wife and held up to public ridicule by the townsfolk yet still proclaimed his love for Gomer and God's love for them. He mirrored the vulnerability of God inherent in unconditional love. We don't know how many people responded, but I know one thing for sure. It's easier to take up a cause led by a fellow human being than to follow someone trying to win the Jesus Christ look-alike contest.

Women Can Play Too: Deborah

I realize this is a controversial area, but I don't feel I should duck it. For too many years men have snidely put down women's ability to lead with a knock of their intelligence or a wisecrack about their stability. Now there's a new breed of joke. I saw a bumper sticker the other day which announced:

God is coming soon

And man is She mad.

I do think it's a serious scriptural issue. That's why I picked Deborah as an example of women in leadership. She was a prophetess, judge, military leader and she didn't do poorly as a song writer when it came time to inspire the people. All of this while she was a wife and mother. This is consistent with the model of a good wife who runs her own business presented in Proverbs 31, only Deborah's business was the nation Israel. Now it's true that there aren't many Deborahs in the Bible. I see this as a cultural quirk rather than obedience to a biblical prohibition.

There's no question that women were relegated to a submissive role as a result of the Fall. Pain at childbirth and hard toil in the fields were also tragic outcomes. But there's no reason to perpetuate the fruit of sin. We don't object to anesthetic during labor or tractors to till the land on theological grounds. Why then gulp hard at a woman giving direction to men?

It may well be that a given group isn't ready to handle female leadership. (We men can be a bit insecure.) I see Paul's admonition about women in charge as accurately reflecting the tenor of his times. At Wheaton College we have our first female student-government president. She's doing a crackerjack job. Folks are now wondering why it seemed like such a big deal at first. Perhaps those of us in leadership posts tend to underestimate the flexibility of our followers. We claim that they're not ready for change. It may be us.

Champion of the Weak: Amos

A few years ago I began reading Scripture. It's a dangerous thing to do. I discovered something that I'd glossed over for a long time. God has a special concern for those on the margins of society: the poor, the hungry, the powerless, the widows, the orphans, the oppressed. If you want to discover this for yourself, read through the Gospel of Luke with a mindset attuned to picking up Christ's compassion for the down and out. Most leaders miss this. They're up and in.

Make no mistake. A leader has power. And most leaders do a credible job of responding to the needs of group members who are intelligent, articulate, wealthy and attractive. It's a great crowd to run with. They share the same background, speak the same language, and wear the mantle of competence with a gentle ease. The weak are harder to love. They're often unable or unwilling to take even the first faltering step toward self-improvement. Yet they are precisely the ones who need leadership, special attention, protection, direction and encouragement. It's been said that the single best indicator of a society's health is the way it treats those who are in dire circumstances. As leaders we often come up short on fulfilling the biblical mandate to share Christ's concern for the helpless. Amos suggests that our callous disregard of that mandate could lead to a date with The Man.

Amos saw the injustice perpetuated by King Jeroboam, his high priest Amaziah and the beautiful people of Israel, and tried to help them see their folly. He wasn't gentle. "They . . . trample the head of the poor into the dust of the earth, and turn aside the way of the afflicted" (Amos 2:7). He called a spade a spade. "Hear this word, you cows of Bashan, . . . who oppress the poor, who crush the needy   Woe to those who lie upon beds of ivory, and stretch themselves upon their couches" (Amos 4:1; 6:4). My guess is the elegant women of Israel didn't appreciate the bovine allusion. "I hate, I despise your feasts, and I take no delight in your solemn assemblies.   But let justice roll down like waters, and righteousness like an everflowing stream" (Amos 5:21, 24)

Amos failed. The power structure of Israel refused to take seriously God's call for the haves to care about the have-nots. But there are times when fidelity to God's example is the best a leader can do. He can lead. The responsibility to follow is up to others.

A Touch of Organization: Nehemiah

As cupbearer to King Artaxerxes of Babylon, Nehemiah was underemployed. One can imagine him organizing the royal wine cellar his first day on the job—dry white wines on the left, the rosé and Burgundies on the right. Stacked by year and region from floor to ceiling; each bottle checked off on an inventory master list. Nehemiah was an organizational whiz.

The expatriot Jew knew a secret that many leaders fail to grasp. If you get sloppy with details, you get sloppy with people. He was able to please the king with excellent service and a cheerful countenance. When it came time to ask for the big favor, the king was hooked.

Not only did Nehemiah get permission to go to Jerusalem to rebuild the wall, he was able to tell the king how long it would take. He had the foresight to ask for letters from the ruler authorizing the work. When he got there he found the city in disarray. It was such an overwhelming task that people were discouraged before they started. So no one started—until Nehemiah organized a defense system with an early warning alert. Men worked with a spear in one hand and a trowel in the other. The work never stopped until the wall was completed fifty-two days later.

Good leaders are people persons, so they tend to badmouth paper work. But details are important. It's only when you start forgetting appointments, missing deadlines and breaking promises that you discover how important they are. Organization probably never made a great leader. But the lack of it certainly brought many down. It's not important what kind of system you use to keep straight all the minutiae of the job, but some kind of system is vital.

I'm fortunate. I tend to think in ordered sequences. You'd

Reprinted from Saturday Review. Cartoon by Peter Steiner.

"Well, men, we've got a heck of a wall to build, so let's get started."

never know it to look at my office—books stacked in the corners, papers all over the desk. But I have a set way of handling mail, phone requests, teaching responsibilities, outside assignments. For me the crucial aid is a wallet-sized combination calendar and address book that is always in my back pocket (unless I'm using it). That and a daily list of things to do is the backbone of my organization. Others thrive on elaborate color-coded filing systems, computer print-outs and work-flow analyses. People need to know their own rhythms and be realistic about what they can handle mentally. But do whatever it takes to manage the work rather than letting it manage you.

There's a lot of almost-but-not-quite leaders who have creative visions, interpersonal skills, and the intellectual prowess of a Rhodes scholar. But they stubbed their toe by simple adminis-trative bumbling. They can't bring themselves to acknowledge that dealing with details is a way of putting wheels on love. The curse ends up on the lips of their people who are no longer theirs.

A Bit of Drama: Elijah

I suppose we shouldn't need spectacle. As Christians we ought to be able to plod along out of appreciation for all God has done. But who wants to be a plodder? There's a bit of racehorse in all of us that's just waiting to break into a full gallop when we see the bright silks, hear the call of the trumpets and sense the excite-ment of the crowd. I believe that this built-in desire for drama is also a gift of God. Nations and groups alike need their Exodus, moon walk, raid on Entebbe or World Cup Championship to rally the troops. As the leader of God's side, Elijah understood that.

He challenged the prophets of Baal to a contest (1 Kings 18). It could have been set up in a sterile laboratory under controlled conditions. But Elijah wasn't looking for verification. He knew who would win. He wanted impact. Everyone loves a contest. Even those who were sold out to Baal couldn't resist the pull of one-on-one competition, winner take all. Whose God could set a sacrifice on fire? He gave Jezebel's priests all the time in the world to pray and plead. When it became clear to the crowd that they couldn't get a spark with a match and a five-gallon can of gasoline, he began to taunt them. Maybe their God was taking a nap or was going to the bathroom. (That's the meaning of the Hebrew in 18:27, and the ridicule drove the false prophets into a frenzy.) The crowd loved it.

When it was his turn he became the master showman. He poured water on the meat and the wood—except he had others do it instead of himself. He didn't want to be accused of sneaking on lighter fluid. And besides, there's nothing like giving others hands-on contact to get them personally involved. Then before he called down God's fire he interpreted the act to the people lest they miss its theological significance. When the suspense was unbearable he stepped aside to let God do what only he could do. Folks remembered that day for a long time.

I learned the power of the dramatic when I was on Young Life staff. Our area had a traditional fall camp the weekend after Thanksgiving. Students stayed away in droves. We were lucky to scare up a crew of fifty, and most were Christians who felt obligated. I decided to try to create an extravaganza that would pull the marginal non-Christian who only came to get out of the house or because his girl was there. We rented an entire ski resort on the bluffs overlooking the Mississippi River (preseason rates) and chartered a train to take us there. The train stopped at the bottom of the hill, and we walked a few steps to the ski lift and were whisked up to the lodge. That had pizzazz. Some signed up just for the fun of getting there.

We billed it as a Greco-Roman weekend. We ran a chariot race in U-Haul trailers, naval battles in the swimming pool, showed the movie *Ben Hur* and called our dinners Roman banquets. Amidst all the fun and foolishness we presented the message that turned the Greco-Roman world inside out. Three hundred came on the weekend, and many made a commitment to Jesus Christ. They all talked about it to their friends, and it became an annual event. No question that this sort of thing can be overdone. Bread and circuses are no substitute for solid guidance. But a flair for the dramatic is a big plus.

Integrity: Abimelech

What in the world is Abimelech doing in this catalog of godly leaders? Here's a heathen king who's about to take Sarah as a mistress. How can I cite him as an example of integrity? Because sometimes worldly people exhibit greater morality than people of faith.

Abraham and Sarah came to the land of Gerar (Gen 20). They told the king that Sarah was his sister (technically correct) but neglected to mention that they were married. Abimelech sent for Sarah, but before he touched her God appeared to him in a dream. "Behold, you are a dead man," the dream began and got worse as God revealed who Sarah was (Gen 20:3). But the king protested mightily. "In the integrity of my heart and the innocence of my hands I have done this" (Gen 20:5). God agreed but said if he didn't return Sarah posthaste, he'd be a goner. Abimelech went one better. He not only restored Sarah to Abraham, he gave him sheep, oxen, servants, one thousand pieces of silver and an offer to stay rent-free anywhere. I see this as a class response from someone who'd received shoddy treatment.

Abimelech acted with integrity. The reason may have been that the dream put the fear of God in him. But that's not a bad motivation for a leader to have. Integrity has to touch all the bases. Sexual purity is one of them, and leaders are particularly vulnerable because of the magnetic effect of power. My working philosophy over the years has been not to worry too much about appearances. If they're prone to gossip, people will speculate and talk regardless of what you do. But I want to make sure that my actual behavior is ethical and aboveboard, and that people know why I do what I do and are free to challenge or question me about my behavior. I would hate to dishonor God, disgrace my group and confuse its members to satisfy a selfish desire.

Many Christian leaders have a tough time being straight with others when it comes to dismissal from a job, rejection of an application or passing on other disappointing news. Sometimes I think the secular world is kinder. Because we want to be loving, we don't always let the other person know they're headed for a fall. We lull them into a false sense of security with smiles, assurances and ducking hard questions. When the ax falls, the leader often denies personal responsibility for the decision. Circumstances, other people or the fickle finger of fate is to blame. The victims are given no warning or recourse. They don't even know where to vent their anger. Often God gets the rap and that's tragic. Integrity means being honest with our people, sharing the true reason for our official actions. I'm convinced that you can tell how Christian an organization is by the way it handles the passing of bad news.

Confidence Is Contagious: Paul

The apostle Paul wrote that we should not have an exaggerated view of our own importance (Rom 12:3). Many leaders take that to mean that it's wrong to take pleasure in their pastoral or organizational skills. They publicly demean their abilities and privately lash themselves whenever they have a taste of success. "Don't thank me. Thank the Lord," they say, leaving the one who paid a compliment feeling slightly dirty. Paul wasn't this way. If anyone had reason to boast, he did. And so he did.

I could have picked Paul to illustrate any number of leadership traits: love, faithfulness, courage or another characteristic. But I'm struck by his bold approach to the Corinthians when they cut down his right to lead. In perhaps the longest New Testament passage on a single topic, he parades the marks of his apostolic authority (2 Cor 10—12). Shipwrecked, left for dead, beaten, blessed with a special vision of Jesus, working without pay, Paul states that he's just as qualified as any spiritual adviser they might have. One gets the impression that he really means he's much more qualified! Sure, he says it's folly, but to deny his divine gifts and calling would be to question God's provision.

I know of no other single trait more necessary for leadership than a large dose of self-confidence. Those who are sure where they're going and set off with a firm step will always draw a crowd. Don't confuse confidence with cockiness. Cockiness is the result of insensitivity or lack of imagination. As the tongue-in-cheek jest suggests, "If you can keep your head while others around you are losing theirs, it's obvious you don't understand the situation." But confidence comes from the inner conviction that you can overcome whatever gets in the way. That conviction can come from the unconditional love of warm parents. It can come from the day-in, day-out experience of doing a job well. It can come from the knowledge that God has tapped you to do his will and that in his power you cannot fail. In any case it's a scarce enough resource that it should not be wasted. Enjoy!

Best When Service Is Greatest: Jesus Again

I just saw an old "Twilight Zone" rerun on TV which picked up on the theme of service. A superior race from another galaxy came to earth offering all sorts of technological goodies to mankind. They freely shared methods of quadrupling food production, secrets of cheap energy and the science of supersonic travel. The aliens even took people to their home planet to visit, though none returned to earth. (Apparently the new planet was paradise.) When asked about their motivation, they simply stated that they wanted to serve man. In fact they often consulted a manual with the altruistic title *How to Serve Man*. Since the visitors could speak the tongues of earth, no humans bothered to learn their language. Finally one linguist made the effort to translate the manual. Then came the shocker. *How to Serve Man* was a cookbook! There was another reason people didn't come back to earth.

That's a rather quirky story to tell at the close of this book. But the point is gruesomely real. Some leaders feed off their group. They see members as existing for their own personal benefit rather than the other way around. Jesus brought the great reversal.

The night before he died, towel in hand, Jesus knelt down and washed the feet of his disciples. He went further than that. He said, "You call me Teacher and Lord; and you are right, for so I am. If I then, your Lord and Teacher, have washed your feet, you also ought to wash one another's feet. For I have given you an example, that you also should do as I have done to you" (Jn 13: 13-15). This is just as much a mandate as his words "This do in remembrance of me" were for the practice of the Lord's Supper. We celebrate communion, but foot washing is a lost art. Of course we no longer walk along dusty roads in sandals, but it's a basic and precious symbol of service.

I introduced the theme of this book by describing a food co-op that a friend, Jessie, and I started in a low-income housing project. This discussion of servant-leadership has brought us full circle. Although Jessie and I provide the initial impetus for the co-op, it's now vital that we put ourselves at the disposal of the tenants. Since they know their needs better than we do, we now take direction from them. It's hard for us to give up our pet ideas and go by their agenda. But that's the nature of servant leadership, a willingness to lay aside the prerogatives of power in order to empower others. I don't find it particularly easy. I doubt if Jesus did.

Said and Done

I have a poster in my office that shows a hippopotamus with his mouth wide open. "When all is said and done," states the caption, "there's a lot more said than done." This is especially true on the subject of leadership. Seeing me or another leader in action with a group for a day or two could be much better than reading eighty thousand words. Then you could decide if there's any wisdom in the advice. As one of my friends put it, "I don't need to read Em's book; I've seen the play." That's not a bad thought on which to end this book. If you're trying to lead a group of people and wonder how it's really going, don't thumb through these pages looking for an answer. Turn to your people and ask them. Leadership isn't a solo activity. You need to work with your people, not on them. People are ends, not means. Leadership is merely a means to meet their needs.

Notes

Chapter Two: Scratching Where They Itch

[1]Robert Bales, "Task Roles and Social Roles in Problem Solving Groups" in *Readings in Social Psychology,* ed. Eleanor Maccoby, T. M. Newcomb and E. L. Hartley, 3rd ed. (New York: Holt, 1958), pp. 437-47.

[2]Malcolm Knowles and Hulda Knowles, *Introduction to Group Dynamics* (New York: Association Press, 1972), p. 61.

[3]Fred Fiedler and Martin Chemers, *Leadership and Effective Management* (Glenview, Ill.: Scott, Foresman, 1974), pp. 73-93.

[4]Robert Bales, "In Conference," *Harvard Business Review* 32 (March-April 1954): 44-50.

[5]Paul Hersey and Kenneth Blanchard, *Situational Leadership* (San Diego, Cal.: Center for Leadership Studies, 1976).

[6]This covenant has drawn heavily upon ideas set forth in those used by the National Presbyterian Church in Washington, D.C. and Faith at Work.

[7]Wm. Fawcett Hill, *Hill Interaction Matrix (HIM) Monograph (Revised)* (Los Angeles: University of Southern California, 1963).

[8]Kurt Lewin, "Group Decision and Social Change" in *Readings in Social Psychology,* p. 210.

Chapter Three: Take Me to Your Leader

[1]E. Jennings, "The Anatomy of Leadership," *Management of Personnel Quarterly* 1 (Autumn 1961): 2.

[2]Marvin E. Shaw, *Group Dynamics,* 3rd ed. (New York: McGraw-Hill, 1979), pp. 326-31.

Chapter Four: Methods of Decision Making

[1]Andre Delbecq, Andrew Van de Ven and David Gustafson, *Group Techniques for Program Planning* (Glenview, Ill.: Scott, Foresman, 1975), pp. 83-107.

[2]Jay Hall, "Decisions, Decisions, Decisions," *Psychology Today,* November 1971, pp. 51-54.

[3]Irving L. Janis, "Groupthink," *Psychology Today,* November 1971, pp. 43 ff.

Chapter Five: Leading a Discussion

[1]Em Griffin, *The Mind Changers* (Wheaton, Ill.: Tyndale, 1976), pp. 5-9.

[2]Jack Gibb, "Defensive Communication," *Journal of Communication* 11 (September 1961): 141-48.

[3]Paul Watzlawick, Janet Beavin and Don Jackson, *Pragmatics of Human Communication* (New York: W. W. Norton, 1967), p. 51.

[4]John Jones and J. William Pfeiffer, eds., *The Annual Handbook for Group Facilitators,* vols. 1-11 (San Diego: University Associates, 1972-82). Lyman Coleman, *Encyclopedia of Serendipity* (Littleton, Colo.: Serendipity House, 1976).

[5]Remember that I'm referring to discussions in which your goal is to stimulate new thoughts and elicit a response, not make a decision.

Chapter Six: Self-Disclosure
[1]John Powell, *Why Am I Afraid to Tell You Who I Am?* (Niles, Ill.: Argus, 1969), p. 12.

[2]Sidney M. Jourard, *The Transparent Self* (New York: D. Van Nostrand, 1964), p. 104.

[3]I. Altman and D. A. Taylor, *Social Penetration: The Development of Interpersonal Relationships* (New York: Holt, Rinehart and Winston, 1970).

[4]Elliot Aronson, *The Social Animal,* 3rd ed., (San Francisco: W. H. Freeman, 1980), p. 257.

[5]Paul Tournier, *The Meaning of Persons* (New York: Harper and Row, 1957), pp. 68-71.

[6]Valerian Derlega and Alan Chaiken, *Sharing Intimacy* (Englewood Cliffs, N.J.: Prentice-Hall, 1975), pp. 23-24, 34.

[7]Sidney Jourard, *Self-Disclosure* (New York: John Wiley & Sons, 1971), pp. 189-91.

[8]Powell, *Why Am I Afraid,* pp. 62-79.

[9]Louise White quoted in W. H. Fitts, *The Experience of Psychotherapy* (New York: D. Van Nostrand, 1965), pp. 55-56.

Chapter Seven: Conflict
[1]Jerome Skolnick, *The Politics of Protest* (New York: Simon and Schuster, 1969), pp. 3-24.

[2]David Augsburger, Lecture delivered to the faculty of Wheaton College, Fall 1977.

[3]David Augsberger, *The Love Fight* (Scottdale, Pa.: Herald Press, 1973), p. 3.

[4]R. R. Blake and J. S. Mouton, "An Overview of the Grid," *Training and Development Journal* 29 (May 1975): 29-37.

[5]George Bach and P. Wyden, *The Intimate Enemy* (New York: Avon, 1970).

Chapter Eight: Persuasion
[1]Herbert C. Kelman, "Compliance, Identification and Internalization: Three Processes of Attitude Change," *Journal of Conflict Resolution* 2 (1958): 51-60.

[2]Griffin, *The Mind Changers,* pp. 27-41.

[3]Martin Buber, "Elements of the Interhuman," trans. Ronald Gregor Smith in *Bridges Not Walls,* 2nd ed., John Stewart, ed. (Reading, Mass.: Addison-Wesley, 1977), pp. 280-92.

[4]Martin Buber, *I and Thou,* trans. Walter Kaufmann (New York: Charles Scribner's Sons, 1970), p 156.

[5]John Stewart, "Interpersonal Communication—A Meeting between Persons" in *Bridges Not Walls,* pp. 10-25.

[6]Sóren Kierkegaard, *Philosophical Fragments* (Princeton, N.J.: Princeton University Press, 1962), pp. 28-45.

Chapter Nine: Deviance
[1]Anthony Doob, "Societies' Side Show," *Psychology Today,* October 1971, p. 48.
[2]Charles Kiesler and Sara Kiesler, *Conformity* (Reading, Mass.: Addison-Wesley, 1970), pp. 24-39.
[3]A. J. Lott and D. E. Lott, "Group Cohesiveness, Communication Level and Conformity," *Journal of Abnormal and Social Psychology* 62 (1961): 408-12.
[4]Stanley Schachter, "Deviation, Rejection and Communication," *Journal of Abnormal and Social Psychology* 46 (1951): 190-207.
[5]Serge Moscovici, "Toward a Theory of Conversion Behavior," in *Advances in Experimental Social Psychology*, vol. 13, Leonard Berkowitz, ed. (New York: Academic Press, 1980), pp. 209-39.
[6]Vernon Allen, "Situational Factors in Conformity" in *Advances in Experimental Social Psychology*, vol. 2, Leonard Berkowitz, ed. (New York: Academic Press, 1965), pp. 136-49.
[7]Leon Festinger, "Informal Social Communication," *Psychological Review,* 57 (1950): 271-82.
[8]Jonathan Freedman and Anthony Doob, *Deviancy* (New York: Academic Press, 1968), p. 60.
[9]Ibid., p. 46.
[10]Robert A. Dentler and Kai Erikson, "The Functions of Deviance in Groups," *Social Problems* 7 (Fall 1959): 98-107.
[11]Bales, "Task Roles," pp. 437-47.

Chapter Ten: Self-Fulfilling Prophecy
[1]O. Pfungst, *Clever Hans (the Horse of Mr. Von Osten); A Contribution to Experimental, Animal, and Human Psychology* (New York: Holt, Rinehart & Winston, 1965).
[2]As told in *Productivity and the Self-Fulfilling Prophecy: The Pygmalion Effect,* (McGraw-Hill Films, 1974).
[3]Robert Rosenthal and L. Jacobson, *Pygmalion in the Classroom* (New York: Holt, Rinehart & Winston, 1968).
[4]Carl Rogers, *On Becoming a Person* (Boston: Houghton Mifflin, 1961), p. 53.
[5]Frederick Herzberg, "Motivation, Morale and Money," *Psychology Today,* March 1968, pp. 42-45.
[6]George Bernard Shaw, "Pygmalion," in *Selected Plays* (New York: Dodd, Mead, 1948), pp. 269-70.